The Art of
INTARSIA
Projects & Patterns

Garnet Hall

Sterling Publishing Co., Inc. New York
A Sterling/Tamos Book

A Sterling/Tamos Book
© 2000 Garnet Hall
Note. Pattern(s) may be copied for the purpose of making project(s).

Sterling Publishing Co., Inc.
387 Park Avenue South
New York, NY 10016-8810

TAMOS Books Inc.
300 Wales Avenue
Winnipeg, MB Canada R2M 2S9

10 9 8 7 6 5 4 3 2

Distributed in Canada by Sterling Publishing Co., Inc.
c/o Canadian Manda Group, One Atlantic Avenue, Suite 105
Toronto, Ontario, Canada M6K 3E7
Distributed in Great Britain and Europe by Cassell PLC,
Wellington House, 125 Strand, London WC2R 0BB, England
Distributed in Australia by Capricorn Link (Australia) Pty Ltd.
P.O. Box 6651, Baulkham Hills, Business Centre,
NSW 2153, Australia

Design A.O. Osen
Photography Jerry Grajewski and Steve Daniels
         grajewski•fotograph.inc, Winnipeg

Printed in China

Canadian Cataloging-in-Publication Data
Hall, Garnet, 1949 –
      The art of intarsia

      "A Sterling/Tamos book."
      Includes index.
      ISBN 1-895569-66-4

1. Marquetry--Technique.   I. Title.
TT192.H348 2000   745.51´2   C00-920100-9

Library of Congress Cataloging-in-Publication Data

Tamos Books Inc. acknowledges the financial support of the Government of Canada through the Book Publishing Industry Development Program for our publishing activities.

NOTE If you prefer to work in metric measurements, to convert inches to millimeters multiply by 25.4.

The advice and directions given in this book have been carefully checked, prior to printing, by the Author as well as the Publisher. Nevertheless, no guarantee can be given as to project outcome due to possible difference in materials and construction and the Author and Publisher will not be responsible for the results.

ISBN 1-895569-66-4

Contents

The ancient art of intarsia was a form of wood inlay where pieces of different woods, cut into thin tiles, were sunk into or laid onto a solid wood base to form a picture or design. The tiles were held in place with glue and any spaces were filled with other pieces of wood cut to fit. The inlaid pieces were then smoothed and polished. The term comes from the Latin verb *interserere*, meaning to insert, but the name intarsia is not much mentioned in woodworking history books. The words inlay and marquetry appear more often. F. Hamilton Jackson, in his book *Intarsia and Marquetry* (London, Sands & Co., 1903), applies the term intarsia to those inlays of wood in which a space is first sunk in solid wood to be afterward filled with pieces of wood or other material cut to fit, while marquetry is the cutting of various shades or colors of wood veneers and arranging them into geometric (parquetry) or pictorial designs. Jackson also mentions that intarsia has older origins than marquetry, probably because of the early lack of tools needed to cut the thin strips of wood veneers. Today both techniques are practiced. Intarsia especially is enjoying renewed interest among woodworkers around the world and has become one of the most popular woodworking crafts.

Some of the earliest designs using inlay techniques have been found in tombs and show the skill of the creators in cutting and shaping wood to form magnificent patterns and shapes. The fine craftsmanship is all the more remarkable since the early civilizations had only primitive toothed blades made from bronze for cutting tools and stone grinders to smooth the wood. Yet the art flourised among early Egyptians, Greeks, and Romans. During the Dark Ages, however, the art of inlay was nearly lost, kept alive only by monks in the cathedrals of northern Italy where they used wood carvings and inlay for decorative panels around the altar or hanging on church walls.

Most historians agree that the rebirth of intarsia carving and inlay took place in the churches in Sienna, Italy, and there is mention of Manuello and his son Parti doing this work on the choir stalls of the cathedral in 1259. As the Renaissance flourished, inlay art began to rival painting as it adopted the new techniques of using shading and color to indicate perspective (*trompe l'oeil*). Local inlay artists embraced this new technique and it was not long before they became so adept and imaginative that they were able to add depth and form to their works creating scenes suggesting textured rocks, stormy skies, and roads fading off into the distance. As inlay art acquired proficiency at perspective, it approached fine painting in its detail and visual appeal. But instead of paint the intarsia artists used various shades and kinds of wood and subtle arrangements of grains to bring their work to life. This inlay art was achieved with such simple tools as a folding pocket knife, a square-handled gouge, and a short-bladed long-handled knife pressed against the shoulder for cutting.

However, by the 17th century the popularity of intarsia was once again declining in Italy and wood inlay techniques were kept alive by

Above Early intarsia artist Antonio Barili (self portrait) using his primitive tools.

Below Panel from door of S. Pietro in Casinense, Perugia, done in 1500s by Fra Damiano, regarded as the greatest intarsia master of all time. The picture looks dimensional because of the choice and placing of wood grains and colors.

furniture craftsmen in Germany, France, Spain, and Britain. Slowly the craft evolved to a more marquetry style, aided by the invention of the fret saw in 1562 and the first veneer slicer in 1818.

Today, intarsia inlay artists have proceeded in new directions and modern intarsia work appears quite different from the work of the old masters. The raising, lowering, and shaping we see now in intarsia work are not as evident in older inlay works. Indeed, modern intarsia assumes the depth and perspective of relief carving. This is made possible because of modern tools and the choices of woods available. Modern intarsia involves selecting appropriate woods of various grains, textures, and colors and cutting out pieces from these woods to fit a prearranged design. The pieces are raised or lowered according to a plan and the finished work is dimensional.

I am one of these modern woodworkers and I share my joy of creating intarsia pictures with a growing number of woodworking enthusiasts around the world. My first contact with this amazing craft was in 1983. A magazine article featured four simple projects that were stack cut, using a marquetry technique in alternating grain. I made a few of the projects and found it interesting. I believed that more of this work was being done but I could never find actual samples until I was introduced to the intarsia work of Judy Gale Roberts and Jerry Booher. Their projects showed different shades and thicknesses of wood which gave the pieces depth and perspective. This is what I had been looking for. I credit these two artists with creating modern intarsia.

This book attempts to introduce modern intarsia art and its related skills to the woodworking enthusiast. There are twenty intarsia projects and they encompass varying degrees of complexity. If you are new to intarsia, begin with a simple project with a minimum number of pieces and once the basic skills are mastered, proceed to more intricate projects. How-to photographs, and step-by-step explanations are provided and techniques are explained and illustrated. Instructions for wood selection and how to handle woodworking tools are given in detail. Patterns are included for all projects. As you work at the projects you'll find that intarsia creation is very rewarding and great fun to do.

Modern intarsia work creates depth and perspective by raising and lowering wood pieces and arranging wood grain and color to fit a prearranged design.

One of the most important features of any craft work is to protect yourself from harm while creating the projects. Any craft that requires the use of power tools can be dangerous and needs special care to prevent injury. When tools are involved with wood, one of the most hazardous aspects is dust inhalation; therefore, along with safety precautions for tool use, an adequate dust collection system is necessary to enjoy crafting without mishap.

Using Tools Safely

1 Read all manuals that come with tools. Observe all manufacturer's suggestions.

2 Leave all guards and shields in place. Have electrical tools properly grounded.

3 Wear eye protection—full face shields are best. Use ear protection.

4 Use push sticks not fingers to guide wood near sharp blades.

5 Keep all equipment sharpened and in good repair.

6 Use well-made tools that come with full safety shields.

7 Keep work area and tabletops clean and dust free to prevent wood from sticking or slipping.

8 Never work when tired. To stay alert stop every hour, shut tool off, rest before returning to work.

9 Do not clear the worktable with your hand while a saw is running. Always shut off the saw before you clean up.

10 If a blade breaks on a scroll saw be sure to keep fingers away from the blade end.

11 Wear proper clothing. Loose-fitting clothes can get caught in tools and cause injury.

Eliminating Dust from the Work Area

Saws and sanders working on wood create sawdust, and fine dust particles can clog machinery and cause accidents. Fine dust also causes serious respiratory problems such as fibrosis which reduces the ability of the lungs to absorb oxygen. Man-made woods such as plywood and MDF (medium density fiber) board contain chemicals, glues, and resins, and some woods can have mold fungus. Any or all of these may be released into the air when wood is cut or sanded. Breathing these in can weaken natural defense systems, get into the blood stream, and cause immediate and long-lasting damage to the respiratory system. Woods such as surinam, rosewood, redwood, mahogany, boxwood, satinwood, teak, ebony, wenge, and Western red cedar contain an allergen called plicatic acid that causes a condition known as red-cedar asthma. To protect yourself from fine dust hazards use a mask, air filtration device, and dust collector. Larger dust particles and wood chips can be shoveled up and do not pose the same danger to the nose and lungs.

Using a mask

Better masks are rated according to their efficiency. Choose from three basic types.

1 Disposable style covers nose and mouth and has one strap or two

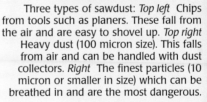

Three types of sawdust: *Top left* Chips from tools such as planers. These fall from the air and are easy to shovel up. *Top right* Heavy dust (100 micron size). This falls from air and can be handled with dust collectors. *Right* The finest particles (10 micron or smaller in size) which can be breathed in and are the most dangerous.

Top left Disposable style
Top right Canister style
Right Full-face style

straps to adjust fit. One strap is not a close fit and is not recommended. The 2-strap style offers minimal protection.

2 Canister style has two canisters on the sides with replaceable filters to filter air as you breathe.

3 Full-face model covers eyes as well. Some models have a hard helmet and belt-mounted powered air supply. This model offers good protection.

Using an Air Filtration Device (AFD)

This cleaning system is an important part of any dust control regimen. It is mounted on the ceiling, has replaceable filters, and cleans the air in the entire shop. Read the manufacturer's instructions to determine the size and style you need. Good air filtration removes 99% of fine micro dust. Some styles have a timer, 2-speed fan, and slot for carbon filter.

Using Dust Collectors

Dust collectors are essential for any serious wood crafter. They come in three basic forms.

1 Shop vacuums are used to pick up debris from floor, workbench, or tools. Some models have a pre-separator for coarse and fine dust but don't usually do a good job with the finest dust. They are limited by their CFM (cubic feet/minute) and size of canister. A pre-separator will increase the capacity. Make one using a garbage can and cyclone lid.

2 Portable (hooks up to each tool temporarily) or dedicated (set up to each tool permanently with ducting) dust collectors come in single stage where chips and dust are drawn through a blower fan into a collection bag or two stage which separates larger debris from dust and collects both separately. Collection bags must be adequate to contain the finest dust so particles do not escape into the air. When setting up the system, the heaviest tools should be closest to the collector. See table for CFM requirements (p7) for various tools. This system can be installed in a separate room to reduce noise and exposure to fine dust particles that may escape from filter bags. The room must be vented. A squirrel cage from a furnace is effective to blow dust outside. A fan vent is needed to allow fresh air in. For proper installation of a dust collector system seek professional advice.

3 Small portable AFDs are new and can be used on a limited basis for the woodworker who does not have much space. Their advantage is that they can be easily moved from one woodworking project to another.

Remember that plastic ducting must be properly grounded (as opposed to metal) because it creates static electricity when dust moves through it. The friction could cause a fire. Run a bare copper wire inside mainline and branches and wrap copper on outside of ducting. Metal ducting is safer but plastic is less expensive and easier to install. Seek information from professionals or specialty books such as *Woodshop Dust Control* by Sandar Nagyszalanczy, Taunton Press and *Dust Collection Basics* by Woodstock International, Inc.

Top Ceiling air filtration device (AFD)

Left Small portable AFD

Below Dust collector hooked to sanding tools

Bottom Dust collector hose pinned to sleeve

Keeping the Work Area Clean

Harmful dust can be minimized by maintaining good housekeeping, creating less dust, and limiting work time exposure. Try these helpful hints.

1 Purchase lumber S4S (smoothed on all four sides) because it requires less planing.

2 Keep blades and bits sharp to produce larger chips, less sawdust.

3 Do not over sand—220-grit paper is often enough.

4 Use hand tools to create less dust (perhaps a scraper instead of a power sander).

5 Use new narrow kerf (notch made by cutting) blades which create 25% less dust.

6 Reduce clutter in the shop, store unused tools in drawers.

7 Store wood in a separate area.

8 Clean up shop regularly.

9 Close in open shelves.

10 Do not sweep shop. Use a shop vacuum or damp cloth for dust.

11 Do dust-making work at end of workday—less time for you to breathe dust in.

12 Take rest breaks away from work area to breathe in fresh air.

13 Sand outdoors if possible.

14 Store dust masks in closed containers.

15 Install remote control to make the system easier to use.

16 Use portable vacuum for access to all parts of shop.

17 Purchase tools with dust collector adapters.

18 Use quick change or magnetic hold downs on hoods and hoses for easy connect/disconnect.

19 Place all sanding tools in one area (isolated if possible) so hook-up to a dust collector will be easier.

20 Wear an apron in the shop to keep clothes clean and leave it in the work area. Wear closed-toe shoes and clean them well before entering living areas.

TOOL	CFM requirements
band saw	400
router/shaper	300
drill press	250
disc sander	300
stationary belt sander	300
floor sweep	400
table saw	300
jointer	350
12 in planer	400
20 in planer	700
radial arm saw	350
oscillating spindle sander	300-500

CFM refers to the amount of suction needed to clear sawdust from the tool.

Example of an adequate, inexpensive sanding area and tool set-up.

These woods present the most health hazard to woodworkers.

TOXIC WOODS

Robert Woodcock, R.N., B.S.N., C.E.N.

REACTION	SITE	SOURCE	INCIDENCE
I—IRRITANT	S—skin	D—dust	R—rare
S—sensitizer	E—eyes	W—wood	C—common
C—nasopharyngeal	R—respiratory	LB—leaves	U—unknown
cancer	C—cardiac	bark	
P—pneumonitis,	N—nausea		
alveolotis (hypersensitivity pneumonia)	malaise		

DT- direct toxin

WOOD	REACTION	SITE	POTENCY	SOURCE	INCIDENCE
Bald Cypress	S	R	+	D	R
Balsam Fir	S	E, S	+	LB	C
Beech	S, C	E, S, R	++	LB, D	C
Birch	S	R	++	W, D	C
Black Locust	I, N	E, S	+++	LB	C
Blackwood	S	E, S	++	D, W	C
Boxwood	S	E, S	++	D, W	C
Cashew	S	E, S	+	D, W	R
Cocobolo	I, S	E, S, R	+++	D, W	C
Dahoma	I	E,S,	++	D, W	C
Ebony	I, S	E,S	++	D, W	C
Elm	I	E, S	+	D	R
Goncalo Aves	S	E, S	++	D, W	R
Greenheart	S	E, S	+++	D, W	C
Hemlock	C	R	?	D	U
Iroko	I, S, P	E, S, R	+++	D, W	C
Mahogany	S, P	S, R	+	D	U
Mansonia	I, S	E, S	+++	D, W	C
Maple (mold)	S, P	R	+++	D	C
Minosa	N	n/a	?	LB	U
Myrtle	S	R	++	LB, D	C
Oak	S	E, S	++	LB, D	R
	C		?	D	U
Obeche	I, S	E, S, R	+++	D, W	C
Oleander	DT	N, C	++++	D, W, LB	C
Olivewood	I, S	E, S, R	+++	D, W	C
Opepe	S	R	+	D	R
Padauk	S	E, S, N	+	D, W	C
Pau Ferro	S	E, S	+	D, W	R
Peroba Rosa	I	R, N	++	D, W	U
Purple Heart		N	++	D, W	C
Quebracho	I	R, N	++	D, LB	C
	C		?	D	U
Redwood	S, P	R, E, S	++	D	R
	C		?	D	U
Rosewoods	I, S	R, E, S	++++	D	U
Satinwood	I	R, E, S	+++	D, W	C
Sassafras	S	R	+	D	R
	DT	N	+	D, W, LB	R
	C		?	D	RS
Sequoia	I	R	+	D	R
Snakewood	I	R	++	D, W	R
Spruce	S	R	+	D, W	R
Black Walnut	S	E, S	++	D, S	C
Wenge	S	R, E, S	++	D, W	C
Willow	S	R, E, S	+	D, W, LB	U
W. Red Cedar	S	R	+++	D, LB	C
Teak	S, P	E, S, R	++	D	C
Yew	I	E, S	++	D	C
	DT	E, S	++++	D, W	C
Zebrawood	S	E, S	++	D, W	R

Courtesy of the Center for Safety in the Arts, New York

Different colors of wood with various grains and textures allow the intarsia artist to create beautiful individual patterns and figures. A great choice of wood is available at saw mills, lumberyards, specialty stores, and mail order through specialty magazines, or you can take a walk through a wooded area and look for unusual fallen pieces. Wood near the crotch of a tree and branch has a swirl pattern, burls form interesting figures, and branches from different tree species yield a variety of grains and colors. The way a board is cut from a log determines the grain pattern. Quarter-sawn boards yield the most grain. No two pieces of wood are ever the same, choose your pieces carefully for the kind of figure you wish to make. Sometimes you need to go through a lumber pile board by board until you find the right piece. Color choice is also important. Woods range from white holly and aspen to red cedar, black ebony and walnut, orange osage to an endless variety of browns and even stripes. Textures range from fine to rough from species to species and even within a variety. How you use wood grain, figure, and texture will make the intarsia project uniquely yours. Knowing about wood can help you make the best selections. Help can be sought from the nonprofit International Wood Collectors Society (IWSC) 2300 Wet Rangeline Road, Greencastle, IN 46135-7875. Or contact them on the internet: e-mail address, cockrell@indy.tds.net; or check their web site at http://www.kiva.net/~rjbrown/w5/iwcs.html. They also publish a monthly journal called *World of Wood*.

Finding Suitable Wood

Left Edge grain *Right* flat grain

Clockwise from top left figured maple, feathered oak, bird's eye maple, lacewood, spalted birch, sycamore, figured cherry, streaked basswood, *center* birch burle

Drying Wood

Moisture content in wood refers to the amount of water relative to its weight. For woodworking, moisture content should not be above 8 percent. Construction grade lumber, which is kiln-dried, is about 18 percent. Therefore most purchased lumber has to be dried for your woodworking needs. Excessive moisture in wood used for woodworking will cause cracking, glue failure, bubbling, or shrinking. Dry the wood purchased using these methods.

1 Dry small green pieces in your workroom. Stack larger pieces six inches off the floor with ¾-in stickers between boards, and away from a wall for good air circulation. When stacked inside, green wood will dry more rapidly. Paint board ends to prevent cracking

2 Larger pieces can be stacked outside off the ground with ¾-in stickers between the boards. Cover the pile with a sheet of plywood and some weight to prevent warping. Be sure to paint board ends to prevent cracking.

Once all the free water has been removed, drying will continue for six months per inch of lumber thickness. Shorter drying time can be accomplished by drawing air through the lumber stack with a fan.

Top left	Top right
wenge	red gum
aromatic cedar	silver maple
bloodwood	black walnut
aspen	spruce
South American walnut	paduak

Western red cedar (called canoe wood, giant arbor vitae, Idaho cedar, Pacific red cedar, shinglewood, and stinking cedar) is most commonly used for intarsia. It is light, soft, and straight-grained. It resists decay and has a beautiful array of textures and shades, from light pinkish to reddish brown and darker. It is readily available and moderately priced. This wood sands easily but needs about three coats of finish for a deep luster. Note the dust from this wood can cause allergies so be sure to observe good dust control (p7). Western red cedar can be used alone or with other woods in a project. See the following list.

WHITE

ASPEN is the first choice for white. Wood is soft and moderately priced. Can be very white or have brown streaks throughout.

SILVER MAPLE (called Mississippi maple or shimmering maple) is harder than aspen. Can be white, pinkish, or streaked with brown flecks. Has a nondescript grain but can have a figure that gives a shimmering look.

SPRUCE (called Adirondack spruce, blue spruce, or skunk spruce) is easy to work. Comes in various shades of white and can have bluish-gray streaks.

PINE (soft white pine or harder yellow pine) is easy to work but has high-pitch content that can plug blades. Can be white or have a bluish steak.

HOLLY is the hardest of the white woods with almost no figure. Must be cut in winter and dried before the hot weather to retain ivory white color. Very expensive and difficult to find.

BLACK

BLACK WALNUT (dark brown to black) is moderately hard, cuts and sands well. Can have interesting figures. Moderately priced.

WENGE (called pallissandre, dikela, or fiboto) is very hard, very black. Can have brown streaks. Expensive and difficult to find.

SOUTH AMERICAN WALNUT (called juglans species, similar to North American walnut) is easy to work, easy to find, but more expensive. Used for contrast.

RED

BLOODWOOD (called Brazil redwood, cardinal wood, muirapirange, pau rainha, palo de sangre, satine rubane) is first choice for a deep dark red color. Very hard, sands well, finishes nicely. To cut with a scroll saw use #9 precision ground (PG) blade and change it often. Requires much sanding. Can be cut with band saw. Expensive and available through specialty hardwood stores.

AROMATIC CEDAR (called eastern red cedar, Tennessee cedar, chest cedar, or red cedar) is pinkish red, often with white streaks or white on one side, red on the other. Boards usually not wider than eight inches. Often have internal stress cracks that promote breaks. Many knots add interest. Soft and easy to cut and shape. Oil content makes it difficult to finish (try non-yellowing finish or latex finish). Readily available, moderately priced.

YELLOW

PAU AMARILLO (called Brazilian satinwood or satina) is first choice for a bright rich canary yellow that holds its color. Hardwood that cuts and sands well. Takes a nice finish. Expensive and available through specialty wood stores.

YELLOW CEDAR (called Alaska cedar, nootka-cypress, nootka false cypress, or yellow-cypress) is usually pale yellow and contrasts with pau amarillo. Wood is soft, easy to work, moderately priced. Grain and figure not outstanding.

Other woods with a pale yellow hue are ponderosa pine, caragana, and some hickory, and orange osage when freshly milled but turns to orange-brown color when exposed to light.

GREEN

AMERICAN YELLOW POPLAR (called tulip tree, canary wood, canoe wood, tulip poplar, white wood, or hickory poplar) is grayish-white but the heart will turn green or gray when exposed to light. Soft, easy to work, readily available, and moderately priced.

SUMAC (called staghorn sumac or velvet sumac) grows as a shrub or small tree no more than five inches in diameter. Not available as commercial wood so you have to find it yourself in northeastern United States and eastern Canada. Resaw it into small boards and glue onto scrap material to get required thickness. Distinctive green color, soft, and easy to work.

VERA WOOD (called maracaibo, lignum-vitae, guayacan, or bera cuchivaro) is a hard waxy wood with green color when exposed to light. Difficult to cut but polishes to a nice finish and needs no further finishing—this green color can be highlighted with durathane finish. Finish pieces before you glue to project. Difficult to find and expensive.

BLUE/GRAY

BLUE MAHOE (called mahoe, mountain mahoe, or seaside mahoe) can have heartwood richly variegated in shades of purple, metallic blue, olive brown. Difficult to find, expensive.

SPRUCE boards can sometimes be found in blue/gray color but you need to search through the pile of boards carefully.

PURPLE

PURPLE HEART (called violet wood, pauroxo, or coracy) is very hard and difficult to cut and sand. Use sharp PG scroll saw blade or use band saw for faster cut. When sanding, stop frequently to allow wood to cool. To shape, start with coarse sandpaper. Expensive, but readily available through specialty stores. Adds color and interest to wood project.

ORANGE

ORANGE OSAGE is fairly hard but cuts and sands reasonably well. Yellow, but turns orangy brown after being exposed to light for a few months. Easy to find. Moderately priced.

AFRICAN PADAUK (called comwood, barwood, corail, yomo, vermilion, bois rouge, African coral wood, or muenge) has heartwood bright orange red to blood red. Easy to cut and shape, has intoxicating odor. Moderately priced and readily available in specialty stores.

SPECIAL EFFECTS

ZEBRAWOOD is pale brown with dark streaks. Easy to work and takes

Top left	Top right
gray poplar	sumac
blue spruce	pau amarillo
yellow cedar	vera wood
zebrawood	orange osage
green poplar	purple heart

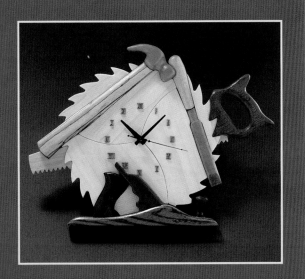

a nice finish. Readily available from specialty stores but very expensive. RED GUM (called sweetgum, alligator tree, alligator wood, liquidamber, hazel pine, sap gum, star-leafed gum, satin walnut, red gum, or belsted) comes in various shades of brown with streaks of red and black. The grain is interlocked in the form of a ribbon stripe and is very beautiful.

For more wood varieties see *Know Your Woods*, Albert Constantine, Jr. (revised 1975), Charles Scribner's Sons, New York; *Native Trees of Canada*, R. C. Hosie, Fitzhenry & Whiteside Ltd., Canada; *A Guide to Useful Woods of the World*, ed. James H. Flynn, Jr., King Philip Publishing Co., Maine; *World Woods in Color*, Willam Alexander Lincoln, Linden Publishing Co. Note   The color and marking of woods often vary within a species and one order of wood that comes into a lumberyard can differ from another. It is best to pick out your own wood from lumber piles, if possible. If not, try to explain the kind of wood, color, and markings as completely as you can to avoid disappointment when it is shipped to you. Exotic wood dealers sometimes offer the most expensive woods in smaller pieces. Choose a dealer whom you like and stay with him. He will get to know what you need.

Tools

Intarsia can be done with simple tools such as a fret saw and some sandpaper, plus patience.

One of the good things about intarsia is that you don't need a lot of fancy tools or a large shop to enjoy this hobby. If all you have is a fret saw and sandpaper, you can create great projects. Of course, power tools make it easier and quicker. I am a great fan of all the latest hi-tech equipment and I think I've tried them all. Yet I've settled on a few tools that take care of all my needs, and surprisingly they are usually the least expensive tools.

Cutting Tools
BAND SAW VS SCROLL SAW
A band saw cuts more quickly than a scroll saw but cannot do the inside cuts that many intarsia patterns require. When you have to cut a shape out of the inside of a board, for example, a scroll saw allows you to drill a hole, disconnect the blade, thread the blade through the hole, reconnect the blade, and cut the shape. A band saw cannot do this, cannot cut as tight a radius, and leaves rough edges, requiring more sanding. Band saws are useful for resawing pieces thinner. Both band saws and scroll saws have their use for intarsia work. However, before cutting with either make sure the blade is square to the table. Do a quick test. Cut a kerf in a scrap piece of wood, shut the saw off, and if the back of the blade slides into the kerf easily the blade is square to the table.

Square-to-table test using kerf
Above left square; *Right* not square

BAND SAW

The faster cutting time of a band saw sometimes offsets other considerations. Use a band saw with $\frac{1}{8}$ in blade with 15 TPI (teeth per inch). A $\frac{1}{16}$ in blade will cut a tighter radius but dulls too quickly and is hard to track. Lower quality blades are better for cutting softwoods. Better blades cut more aggressively and tend to overcut. Cut hardwoods when the blade is new and cut cedar when the blade is duller.

Cutting a tight radius (less than $\frac{3}{8}$ in) with a band saw is difficult. The blade waivers as it dulls and if you try to cut at the same speed the bottom of the piece will be larger than the top. This will affect the fit so be sure to check the edge of the pieces for square. To cut a small radius, cut in sections, as shown.

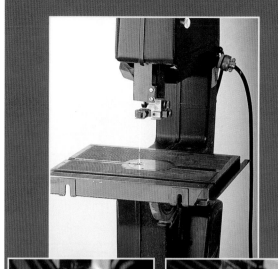

Band saws leave splinters or burrs on the bottom edge of the pieces because the blade cuts in only one direction. This can cause fitting

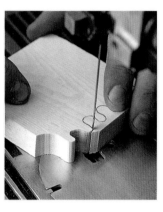

problems and requires careful checking and sanding. Blade guides kept tight to the blade help prevent the blade from twisting and going off line. Choose guide blocks that tighten right to the blade. Those made of fiber products (commercial blocks) are less likely to dull the blade than the steel guide blocks that come with the saw or you can make your own guide blocks out of oily wood such as teak or padauk. They don't last as long as commercial blocks, but can be run very tight to the blade without any danger of dulling the teeth or causing sparks, plus they are easy to resurface and cheaper than the cool blocks commercial variety.

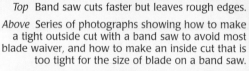

Top Band saw cuts faster but leaves rough edges.

Above Series of photographs showing how to make a tight outside cut with a band saw to avoid most blade waiver, and how to make an inside cut that is too tight for the size of blade on a band saw.

Right Band saw guides, properly adjusted, help prevent blade from twisting and going off line.

Band saws leave a wider kerf so the fit is a bit looser than a scroll saw cut. However, a band saw will do the job faster for production work.

SCROLL SAW

Scroll saws are my preferred cutting tool for intarsia. These saws come in a wide range of sizes, shapes, and qualities. Useful options include quick no-tool blade changes and variable speed. Purchase the best saw you can afford and one you can handle comfortably.

Above Homemade guide blocks work well and are easy to make.

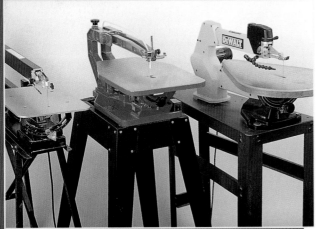

Blades are important in scrolling. Most blade styles come in a wide range of sizes from 00 to 12. The size designations are not universal, but generally the smaller the number the smaller the blade. The best blades for cutting intarsia woods are precision ground (PGT) or super sharp style blades. They come in three sizes, 5, 7, and 9 (7 is used most often). These blades can handle any ¾-in hardwood and Western red cedar, leaving smooth edges that require less sanding. Since they are a reverse-tooth blade there is no deburring to do. The reverse teeth cut on the up stroke and leave a clean bottom. Although a scroll saw cuts more slowly than a band saw it saves time because it requires less sanding. Learn to operate the scroll saw at its fastest speed. If the saw vibrates badly, slow down or bolt the saw to a solid surface.

Note PG blades cut too aggressively for thin (less than ⅜ in) material. Use #3 crown-tooth or double-tooth blades which are less aggressive in thin material.

Top Typical scroll saws

Right A safety fence is recommended when using a scroll saw. We have removed it for photographic purposes.

Below Drill press and jigsaw

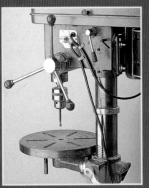

You will need something to drill holes for eyes and inside cuts. Use a drill press or an electric drill if you have a steady hand. A saber or jigsaw is useful for cutting boards down to size, making it easier to handle them on a band or scroll saw.

Shaping and Sanding Tools

The "sandpaper carving" stage of intarsia requires a variety of sanding tools depending on the complexity of the piece. Adapt the tools you have and add others as needed. The method below eliminates hand sanding and greatly reduces production time.

1 Use a small 1-in diameter by 4-in long pneumatic drum sander for the initial shaping and much of the sanding. Air pressure in the drum is adjustable. When the pressure is reduced the sander becomes softer and forms over the pieces giving a smooth chatter-free finish, making a smooth transition from one level to the next.

Note The drum can also be used in a drill press or small hand drill as well as in power carvers such as Foredom or Dremel.

2 Use a flap sander for the final sanding. Hand sand only very small pieces.

Large pneumatic sander   6-in portable belt sander

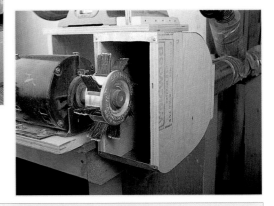

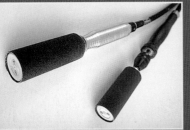

Above A flap sander does most finish sanding.

Far left Small pneumatic drum sander chucked into flex shaft, power carver, or small drill, has become my favorite tool.

Right Larger drum sander chucked into a ⅜ in drill

Wood Burning Tools for Special Effects

Wood burning adds interesting detail to projects. Mark the burn lines on the project pieces lightly with a pencil and burn them in with a good wood burning tool. Use either a large or medium skew-shaped tip. Lightly sand off any remaining pencil marks. Be sure work area is free of sawdust and wood chips before beginning the burning.

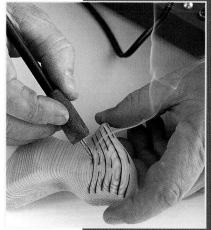

Enlarging Patterns

The patterns in this book are smaller than the actual project size and must be enlarged.

1 Photocopy pattern, enlarging it to the required size.

When using small sheet copiers, enlarge pattern in sections and tape sheets together. If sheets do not align it may be because photocopiers have a margin of error of 1 to 2 percent.

2 Have the pattern photocopied by a firm that specializes in copying blueprints.

They have large copiers that produce accurate, one sheet copies up to 36 in wide and any length.

Transferring the Pattern to Wood

Once the pattern has been enlarged and the various shades of wood chosen you are ready to transfer the pattern to the wood. There are three ways to do this.

1 Tracing the pattern onto wood

Place the pattern onto the piece of wood you wish to cut out, being careful to find the desired grain and shade. Hold one edge of the pattern firmly and slip a piece of carbon paper under the pattern. Trace around the piece you want to cut out with a sharp pencil or ballpoint pen. Be accurate because this is the cutting line and pieces must fit. Where two pieces touch follow the same line exactly, as shown at top. Pattern is reusable three or four times.

2 Making a template

Make a template of the pattern using materials such as ⅛-in Baltic birch (lucan) plywood, acrylic, lexan, or MDF board. Baltic birch is preferred because it has no veneer voids and will hold together when cut into small pieces. Place the pattern onto the wood, tape (use masking tape)

Working with Patterns

Tracing a common line on a pattern onto wood. Be sure to trace on the same line where the pieces touch. Procedure is the same whether this is the actual intarsia piece or a wood template.

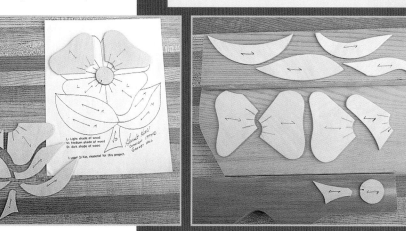

Templates are cut out, ready to trace onto woods chosen for project pieces.

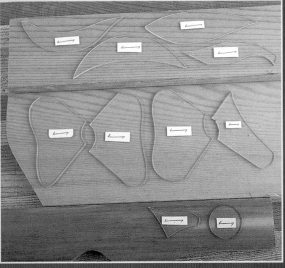

Pencil/pen position is important when tracing around a template. Make sure the point of the pencil/pen is at the point were the template meets the wood (at a 45° angle), not straight up and down, for accurate fit.

corners and slip a piece of carbon paper under the pattern. Trace the entire pattern onto the wood. Cut out the pattern on the line with a scroll saw (use #3 or #5 double or regular tooth blades with saw running at 1000 SPM (strokes per minute). When template is cut out, mark on it all the grain direction instructions, shade suggestions, thickness pieces should be, and information about fitting that could be helpful when cutting additional pieces. Clean up the edges and backs of templates with sandpaper (a reverse-tooth blade will help keep fuzzies to a minimum). Template is ready to trace onto wood. Store template pieces in a pizza box and mark on the front which pattern it is.

Templates provide good fitting and help in laying out the pieces to make better use of the material. To make two matching projects, turn the template pieces over and make a reverse image of the original. Trace with pencil held at a 45° angle.

Note Acrylic templates have an advantage over plywood templates because the wood grain can be seen through them making it easier to place the pattern to best advantage. Use ⅛-in acrylic with a paper backing and leave the paper on until cutting is finished and edges have been smoothed with sandpaper. Trace the enlarged pattern directly onto the acrylic with carbon paper. If you use poly-covered acrylic rub the cutting blade with a lube stick or run a bead of oil on the cut line so blade won't stick, or remove the poly covering and tape the cut line with masking tape. Use a scroll saw carefully so the acrylic won't melt from the friction of the saw blade (#5 precision blade or #5 or #7 double or skiptooth blade at speed of 800-600 SPM). Once the pattern is cut out any acrylic that has melted and puddled on the edges can be cleaned off with coarse sandpaper (80 or 100 grit). Finally remove the paper backing.

It is also possible to make templates out of thinner ¹⁄₁₆-in plywood or plexiglas, but it requires careful cutting since smaller pieces tend to splinter. Plexiglas can be purchased from any window or windshield repair shop. Lexan stencil blanks can also be used to make templates. Spray glue the pattern onto the stencil blank and cut out the pieces

Template pieces enable you to make better use of the material. Lay them out on the boards you need, move them around to get maximum use of the wood.

Acrylic templates have an advantage over wood templates because wood grain can be seen through them.

with scissors. Number pattern pieces and template pieces to match. Lexan stencil blanks may be purchased at craft supply stores and are the least expensive template material. They store easily in an envelope.

3 Spray gluing pattern to the wood

Cut out each pattern piece carefully and spray glue them onto the wood using a temporary adhesion glue used to attach scroll patterns to wood. Cut out pieces with a scroll saw, cutting just to edge of paper, leaving paper intact.

Spray glue pattern pieces onto wood with a light adhesive so they can be removed later. Not all spray adhesives behave in the same way, so experiment with the amount of spray and the timing.

Intarsia pieces should fit together well and this is easier if the cutting has been carefully done. A saw kerf or $\frac{1}{16}$ inch between pieces is acceptable; however, the closer pieces fit together the better the finished project will look since large gaps distract the eye from the overall aesthetic effect. Some intarsia enthusiasts prefer an airtight fit, but a slight gap does not mean a fitting disaster.

Here are some helpful hints for fitting.

1 Mark boards you have cut pieces from in case you have to remake a piece. You will want to blend in the correct shade so it will fit the design of the project.

2 When using the template method, cut out on the line. This leaves the pieces slightly larger than needed, but it's easier to make the pieces smaller, to fit, than it is to make them larger.

3 When cutting, make sure the blade of the saw is square to the table. (*See* kerf test, p12.) Cut out the piece as carefully as you can. Follow the line and take your time. Careful cutting will reduce fitting problems.

4 If you use a band saw, deburr (sand by hand) the bottom of the pieces before checking for fit. If you use a scroll saw with a reverse-tooth blade, there won't be any burrs.

5 If the blade waivers, you are forcing the saw or cutting too fast and the blade may go off the line. Check the edges of cut pieces with a square to see if the bottom of the piece is larger than the top, then turn them over, find the right template piece and turn it over, and draw on any difference and recut. Correct blade waiver with an oscillating spindle sander (as shown at right) or a drum sander chucked into a drill press (p14). After marking on the bottom of the piece where it is too large, sand to this line with the sander. The piece will be upside down on the table. Make sure the drum is square with the table.

6 After preliminary checking, reassemble the project and check for fit again. Look into the space between the pieces and mark where they touch and have to be trimmed. Trim with a saw, oscillating spindle, or drum sander. The oscillating spindle sander is useful to remove a very small amount of wood. Use a lightbox (p18) to check fit.

7 Fit two pieces by running a scroll or band saw blade down the joint between the pieces. This requires a steady hand, a smooth-running machine, and some experience. It works best on long straight or gently curved joints and not as well on small irregular joints. When joining pieces of irregular shape, set the blade into the inside corner, with the

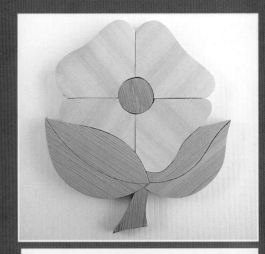

Finished intarsia flower (p28) shows an overall fit of less than $\frac{1}{16}$ inch between pieces.

Check the edges of the pieces to make sure they are square.

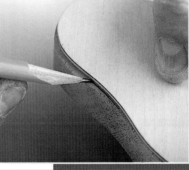

Above Mark on the bottom of piece where it is too large, sand to this line.

Right An oscillating spindle sander or a sanding drum in a drill press are used for squaring edges.

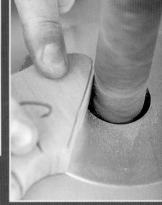

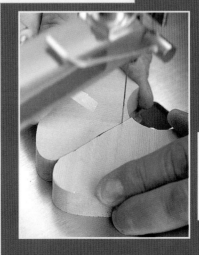

Cutting down the joint between two pieces is a quick way to fit them together.

Cutting down the joint between very jagged pieces.

saw turned off, and set the second piece in place. Then turn saw on and cut down the joint. Turn saw off and separate pieces. Keep doing this until the two pieces fit.

8 Another fitting technique is to cut out pieces and use them to trace common lines with adjoining pieces. Trace the rest of the piece. Cut second piece out and use both pieces to trace a common line with adjoining pieces. Cut out a third piece for three common lines. Continue in this manner. This will improve fit.

9 To ensure fit on larger frame projects, leave a space of $\frac{1}{16}$ in (saw kerf width) between the pieces. Try to fit in frame. If the project is still too large for the frame, reduce larger gaps while continually checking the frame. If fit is impossible for a piece, remake the piece. Find the template, trace it onto the correct shade of wood, and freehand draw where to make the piece larger. Cut it out, try the fit again, and trim to fit.

10 Generally, if you are very careful with the cutting step, fitting is much easier. Mark on the pizza storage boxes for the templates where the pieces didn't fit so you will know where to make it smaller or larger next time.

This flower is reassembled on a lightbox. Look down between pieces and mark with a pencil where they need to be trimmed for a better fit.

Making a Lightbox

Make box from $\frac{3}{4}$-in exterior plywood 19 in wide x 24 in long x $3\frac{1}{2}$ in deep (deep enough for the light fixture) and assemble with $1\frac{1}{2}$ in wood screws or $\frac{1}{2}$ in nails. Butt joints on corners with glue. Attach 20-in long light bar to bottom of box. Run cord out through side of box. Place hole in box near switch for light source which can be shut off without unplugging. Attach $\frac{1}{8}$ in plexiglas to the top with $\frac{1}{2}$ in #4 screws. Pre-drill holes and countersink them, so the screw heads will be flush with the surface of the plexiglas. Use four screws down each side.

Note Translucent plexiglas is also available and prevents glare.

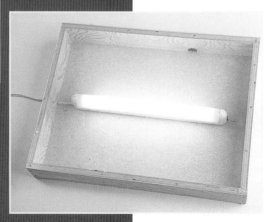
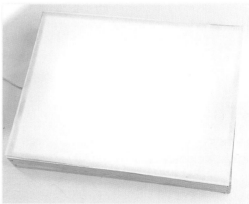

After pattern pieces are cut out and fitted, raise or lower the pieces as marked on the pattern. This technique gives projects a three-dimensional effect, resembling relief carving. All the patterns in this book are based on ¾-in thick base material. The letters **R** and **L** designate raise and lower, and numbers designate the various levels. If a piece has no number designation it will be ¾ in thick. All raising is added to this thickness and all lowering is removed from this thickness.

Raising Pieces

Glue a raiser board to the bottom of each piece that is to be raised. Raise in increments of ⅛ in, so use ⅛ in and ¼ in plywood (scraps) or some of the same wood piece was cut from to make raiser boards. Using the same material gives a better appearance to the finished project if the raised piece is on the edge of the project or the surrounding wood is lower.

For **R**   glue on ⅛ in plywood
   R1 glue on ¼ in plywood
   R2 glue one piece of ⅛ in and one piece of ¼ in to equal ⅜ in
   R3 glue two pieces of ¼ in to equal ½ in
   R4 glue two pieces of ¼ in and one ⅛ in to equal ⅝ in

Attaching Raiser Board

Place piece to be raised onto the raiser board and trace around it. Cut the raiser piece out, cutting inside the line (raiser board is smaller).

If the raiser board is flat, contact glue it to the project piece without clamping unless raiser piece is on the edge of project. Alternatively, glue all the pieces for the same raise onto the appropriate raiser board, allow to dry, then cut out by setting the saw at a 15 degree angle. To raise entire sections where pieces are to be raised the same amount, make one raiser board for all. *See* photograph opposite for details of this technique. Also works for lowering pieces the same amount.

Lowering Pieces

To lower the pieces, resaw the pieces thinner. All patterns in this book are lowered in increments of ⅛ in.

For **L**   cut off ⅛ in
   L1 cut off ¼ in
   L2 cut off ⅜ in
   L3 cut off ½ in
   L4 cut off ⅝ in

Use a band saw for resawing hardwood pieces thinner. Make a simple removable fence to help guide piece. A scroll saw can be used for resawing cedar pieces thinner than two inches. A PG #9 blade works best for resawing. If the piece is thicker than two inches and you don't have a band saw, plane the material thinner. It's possible to resaw on a table saw but *use push sticks* to feed wood and keep fingers away from the blade. It is also possible to sand the pieces thinner. A belt sander with a 50- or 80-grit belt works best.

When resawing on a band saw the wider the blade and the

Trace project piece onto raiser board. Cut out inside the line so raiser board is smaller than the piece and won't interfere with the fit.

Glue all pieces to be raised the same amount onto a common raiser board. If the raiser board is kept flat it should not be necessary to clamp the pieces.

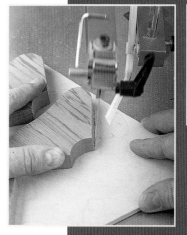

Set scroll or band saw at a 15° angle and cut out pieces. Cut along the point were the piece and the raiser board meet.

Band saw blades do not always track as well as they should so a movable fence allows you to compensate.

fewer the teeth the easier it is to cut through thick or hard material. I use a ³⁄₈ in blade on my old 12 in band saw, with 5 TPI. A ½ in blade would be better but I don't want to put the extra pressure on the old saw and ³⁄₈ in has proven to be more than adequate for my needs.

Using Marking Guides

It is helpful to make marking guides to inscribe lines on the pieces to be resawn (lowered). The guides shown below will fit into most shapes for marking purposes. These four thicknesses (⅛ in, ¼ in, ³⁄₈ in, ½ in) enable me to mark all the thicknesses I use. For example, starting with ¾ in base material, the ⅛ in marker makes **L** and **L4**. Mark the piece to be lowered. Cut on the inside of the line to leave ⁵⁄₈ in of material for **L**. Cut on the other side of the line to leave ⅛ in for **L4**. Marker guides can be made any shape. A square and ruler can also be used to mark cutting lines.

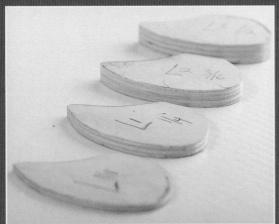

Left A set of four thicknesses marking guides are used to mark pieces to be lowered. This shape seems to fit most situations.

Right The ⅛ in marker gives **L** or **L4**.

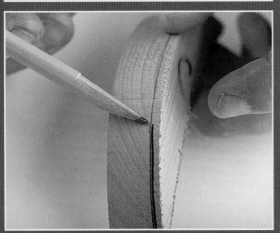

Left Starting with ¾ in base material, cut on one side of the line to remove ⅛ in and leave ⁵⁄₈ in for **L**.

Right Cut on the other side of the line to leave ⅛ in for **L4**.

Use a marking guide or a square to inscribe a line for lowering pieces.

After wood selection, shaping is the next important step in creating a unique intarsia project. It is the step that shows personal style and is labor intensive. The tools you select to do this job will affect the look of the finished project.

As previously mentioned, the small pneumatic sanders and the flap sander virtually eliminate hand sanding. For shaping inside corners and smaller pieces a small hard rubber drum (½ in diameter, 2 in long) sander in a power carver works well. For long pieces use a larger pneumatic sander or a 6 in by 48 in belt sander. Routers are not recommended for shaping intarsia. They can be dangerous when routing very small pieces, and they produce pieces that look machine made instead of handmade.

Using Reference Lines

To help achieve a smooth transition from one level to the next, try to imagine how the project would look in real life or refer to pictures. After all the pieces have been raised and lowered, reassemble the project. Draw reference lines freehand to show how far down to sand each piece to make the desired transition from one piece to another. Each pattern will have different shaping.

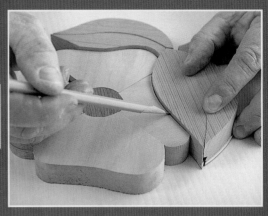

Draw reference lines to guide shaping. Do not shape below reference lines.

Shaping the Pieces

After raising and lowering the pieces, reassemble the project and prepare for shaping. Make sure your dust collector system is on and wear a dust mask because this step creates fine sawdust. Shaping is a creative part of intarsia that depends on individual taste and experience in crafting. Use the photograph as a guide to how the pieces might look. Shaping styles vary from one individual to the next and often depend on the look you are trying to create.

Rose shows different shaping styles in one project.

Left Flower is flat with rounded edges and has little shaping and no raises.

Right Flower and leaves flat and softly rounded

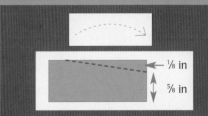

Top Patterns are marked to indicate shaping from one level to another.

Bottom Example: sand/shape edge of piece down to **L**.

Left Petals flat, slightly rounded, leaves raised

Middle Petals dished out to the center, much shaping

Right Unusual shaping

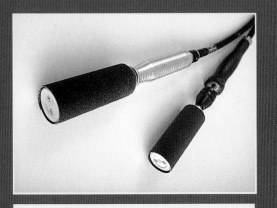

These pneumatic sanders are my main shaping and sanding tools.

Small pneumatic drum sanders used with a flex shaft attached to a motor mounted on the wall make it easier to achieve a smooth transitional shape from low to high pieces. They can also be used in power carvers. Hard rubber sanders usually make hard, angular edges and leave chatter marks. Flap sanders aren't as good for shaping, but are useful for sanding irregular shapes, saving much hand work. The flap sander is also good for texturing pieces. This sander will sand away the soft part of the grain on softwoods such as cedar and pine to create a ripple effect. A combination of tools helps to create a variety of effects, although sandpaper alone can be used to shape softwoods such as cedar.

Since these small sanders are pneumatic, you can put more or less air in them, making them harder or softer for your needs.To begin shaping, use an 80-grit sleeve and pump the sander hard to remove material

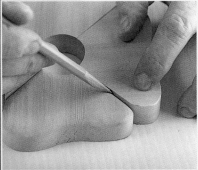

quickly and do most of the shaping. As each piece is shaped keep the project pieces together to continuously check reference lines (see

Top left Sand to eliminate flat edges.

Middle Check for smooth transitions.

Right Example of how to round pieces over to achieve a smooth transition from one level to the next.

Above For finish sanding, releasing some air from the sander allows sander to form well over the piece.

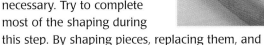

above) and mark new ones if necessary. Try to complete most of the shaping during this step. By shaping pieces, replacing them, and comparing them to surrounding pieces, you will work steadily toward the desired effect. Try to achieve a smooth transition from one level to the next, unless the piece is meant to stand out directly from the other pieces. Exposed flat edges are not attractive. If these are part of the design, sand off any saw marks on the exposed edges and try to achieve a rounded shape, as shown.

To shape pieces as a unit, temporarily attach (use hot glue gun or double-sided tape) the pieces to a scrap piece of backing material, as shown, and use a large pneumatic drum sander for shaping.

Remove from backing and place pieces into the project. This technique works well for shaping the body of animals, birds, or tree trunks.

Project pieces are temporarily glued to a piece of scrap and sanded as a unit.

Sanding
When the initial shaping is completed, begin the finish sanding. Let

some air out of the sander and switch to a 120-grit sleeve so that when you push on the sander it forms well over the piece. Then use a 220-grit sleeve and touch up each piece for any fine scratches or other flaws. As a final step, sand each piece with a flap sander.

Shaping and Sanding Step Guide

1 Assemble the project pieces.
2 Mark on reference lines.
3 Shape pieces with an 80-grit sleeve to the reference lines but not below.
4 Reassemble pieces and check shaping.
5 Draw more reference lines as necessary and check for flat edges, saw marks, and other areas that need sanding. Shade in these areas with a pencil and mark clearly to show where to sand to add more definition.
6 Shape pieces with the 80 grit again.
7 Reassemble pieces.
8 Check and mark areas that require attention, looking again for flat edges, saw and sanding marks. Shape and sand with a 120-grit sleeve.
9 Reassemble pieces.
10 Check again for flat edges, sanding any saw marks, and mark as necessary.
11. Finish sanding with a 220-grit sleeve.
12 Reassemble pieces and check once more for missed pencil marks.
13 Run hand lightly over the project to check for smooth transitions.

Shaping adds realism to a project.

Once shaping and sanding are finished, the next step is to glue the project to the backing material. The best backing material is baltic birch plywood (Swedish or lucan plywood). This better grade, solid core plywood is without voids and has alternating layers of birch veneer as the core, with a veneer covering. It is very stable and less likely to warp (second choice for backing is ordinary oak or birch plywood). Use ¼-in thick plywood (⅜ in for larger projects). Keep the backing material flat and clamping will not be necessary.

Backing and Glue-up

Backing Steps

1 Assemble all fitted, shaped, and sanded pieces onto backing material in correct pattern layout.
2 Trace around project, then remove the pieces.
3 Cut out using method 1 or 2.

METHOD 1
1 Draw another line ⅛ in inside the traced line, as shown, and cut on this line.
2 Assemble pieces on backing so they overlap the edges of backing evenly all around.
3 Use this method if you wish to use a gel finish.

METHOD 2
1 Cut on the line already traced.
2 Assemble pieces on backing to fit evenly out to the backing edges.

Glue-up

1 With project assembled on backing, glue one piece

Tracing the project onto the backing material. Be sure to hold the pieces firmly while you trace.

Method 1 Draw line ⅛ in smaller than project.

Left Method 1 The back is cut smaller than project.

Right Method 2 The back is brought out to edge of project and rounded back.

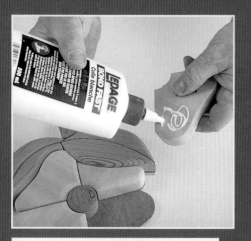

Glue a piece and set it in place. Be sure to even out the space at this point.

at a time, beginning with an outside piece. Place a small amount of glue (use white carpenter's glue which allows 10 to 15 minutes to adjust pieces) on bottom not sides of lifted piece and set back in place. Repeat this step for all pieces, making sure the project is spaced correctly. Allow to sit for 30 minutes after gluing.

Note On large projects glue pieces around the outside to form a frame, then work toward the center. Glue one piece at a time and adjust as you proceed.

2 Long pieces tend to lift off backing at the ends so these pieces may require clamping. Place a scrap of wood on the piece to protect the surface. Allow glued piece to sit for 5 minutes before you apply the clamps, to reduce likelihood of glue creeping. Clamp for 30 minutes. Remove clamps.

3 If you used method 1 to cut backing, you are finished. If you used method 2, edges require chamfering (beveling) or rounding on the back. Use a router and a ⅜-in rounding overbit or a small pneumatic drum or a belt sander. Inside corners are best done with a small hard rubber sander.

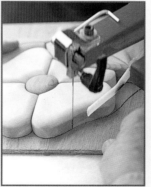

Above left Compass points can be helpful to pick out pieces from the center of a project for gluing.

Middle Project assembled on the backing material. Use scraps to protect the surface on long pieces requiring clamping.

Above and left A router can be used to round over the back in method 2. Use a ⅜-in rounding overbit.

For inside corners use a small hard rubber sander.

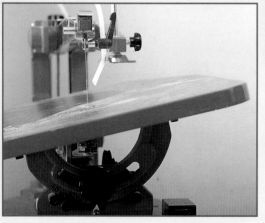

An alternative way to cut out the backing for method 2. Set scroll saw at a 20° angle and cut out the back once all pieces have been glued onto the backing material. This can be difficult. Be careful on tight corners not to damage the work.

Alternatively, glue pieces onto a back ½ to 1 in larger than assembled pieces in case you have to clamp. Cut out with scroll saw (left).

4 Find the center, as shown. Attach a 2-in sawtooth hanger to the back.

Finding the central point to attach the hanger on a large irregularly shaped piece can be difficult. It is best to use a compass point. For smaller projects hold project between thumb and finger, below left, moving the project around until you find the center.

Middle A compass point is used to find the center of larger projects. Get as close as you can by hand and then use the compass to find the exact center point.

Right Use 2-in sawtooth hangers which allow the piece to be hung at different angles.

Any finish made for wood will work for intarsia. You can use durathane, polyurathane, urathane, varnish, lacquer, tung oil, linseed oil, beeswax, latex, and non-yellowing type finishes. They come in wax, paste, gel, and liquid forms and can be sprayed, brushed, wiped, and used for dipping. A variety of lusters usually includes satin (low gloss), semi gloss, and high gloss. The selection of finish is your choice, but here are a few words of caution.

Finishing

1 A wax/gel finish must be applied to the pieces before glue-up. If you apply it after glue-up the finish gets into the grooves and can be difficult to clean up. Use backing method 1 for gel finish (p23).
2 Another problem that arises when you apply a finish before glue-up involves clamping. Clamps may damage the finish so use clamp pads for protection.
3 If you use a liquid finish (varnishes or polyurethanes) you can apply it after the project is glued-up. This method is faster and gives as good a finish as applying finish to pieces separately, although care must be taken to get finish onto the inside edges of pieces as much as possible. If you dilute the first coat with 10 percent thinner the finish will penetrate the grooves and end grain more completely.
4 Most people prefer satin or semi-gloss finish. High gloss makes the wood look like plastic. Most of the paste, gels, and wax type finishes are low luster.
5 Oil-base finishes such as varathane, durathane, and polyurethane have an amber tint. This brightens the color of woods and makes black walnut look blacker and all shades of Western red cedar slightly darker.
6 If you don't want the color of a wood to change, as with white woods, use a non-yellowing finish, such as water-base latex.
Finish pieces separately before gluing-up so white woods will look as white as possible. Use a non-yellowing clear liquid tone finish that

Applying a paste/gel finish to pieces.

Compare two finishes for yellowing of a white wood.
Left latex *Right* oil

Spraying on a finish using a carousel.

Use a vacuum with a brush end to clean a project before applying a finish.

Wipe brush off on can rim and run "dry" brush around edge of project piece.

doesn't change the color of wood and is easy to apply. Usually it has a very strong odor and requires acetone to clean the brushes.

7 A clear latex finish preserves the color of a wood such as aspen. These water-base finishes are odorless and safe to use. Brushes clean up easily in water. However, the water base raises surface wood fibers which necessitates more sanding. Try wiping the wood with a damp cloth before applying the finish, allow to dry, and then sand smooth.

8 A number of finishes come in aerosol cans. To use, follow manufacturer's directions. Be sure to wear a mask rated for finish mists. Spray systems such as Low Pressure High Volume reduce overspray and are a fast way to finish a number of projects. Sprays also have the advantage of less running. Move the spray over the piece in one swipe and don't start or stop spraying while on the piece. Be sure to cover every spot. Placing the piece on a carousel as you spray makes it easier to check all sides.

Preferred Finishing Method

1 Apply three coats of finish to the front of the project and one to the back, sanding between coats. Do not apply too much finish. It will run and leave brush marks. Brush on finish with the appropriate 1-in wide brush: a) natural bristles for solvent-based finishes or finishes that require solvent to clean brush such as varnish, durathane, shellac, and lacquer, or b) synthetic bristle brushes that can be used for both types of finish (solvent and water base).

Be sure to clean brush thoroughly immediately after use. Dip the brush in the solvent and work it into the bristles. Use one container for the initial cleaning and a second container of cleaner solvent for the final cleanup.

2 Apply finish at room temperature. If the air is too warm the finish will dry too quickly and leave bubbles on the surface. If the air is too cool the finish won't dry completely and be difficult to sand smooth. Don't shake the finish can before opening, This incorporates air bubbles into the finish that dry on the surface. Stir gently with a stick. It's best to have a dust-free finishing room that also isolates finish vapors from your other work area. Wear a mask rated for dust as well as vapors. If possible vent your finishing room.

3 Make sure surface of project is dust free. Vacuum project. A brush end for your shop vacuum works well. A tack cloth will also work. Then apply Minn Wax durathane, satin finish, using a mixture of 10% thinner for the first coat which I apply liberally (thin coat soaks in well and won't run). Wipe the brush off on the can rim and run the "dry" brush around the edge of the piece to insure there are no runs on the back of the piece.

5 Allow to dry and then hand sand the surface with 120-grit sandpaper. Vacuum off the piece with the brush end and make sure the piece is dust free.

6 Apply second coat full strength but sparingly. Dip brush in finish and wipe one side on rim of can. Spread this amount of finish as far as it will go and still cover. Allow to dry.

7 Finish the back. If finish has run on the edge, sand it smooth and apply a light coat of full strength finish. Run the brush dry, wipe both sides on the can rim, and run it around the edge. Allow to dry.

8 Apply a final (third) coat full strength to the front. Sand with 220 grit and wipe or vacuum off the dust. Coat should be applied sparingly. Dip the brush in finish 1 in and wipe both sides on finish can. Then dry brush (wipe both sides of brush on can rim a number of times) the edges to eliminate runs.

Experiment with different lusters to add more perspective to a project, such as finishing one side of the object with a high gloss and the other side with a low luster. A touch of high luster finish to the eyes of projects adds life to them. Adding different lusters is time-consuming and best done with a small brush.

Trout oil base high gloss finish

Rose gel matte finish

Simple flower oil base satin finish

Dolphins body—gel matte finish
eyes—high gloss finish

Simple Flower

This simple flower has only ten pieces that fit in straight lines or gentle curves. The center is slightly more difficult to fit. The techniques to make the flower are described in detail. Refer to this project for basic instructions and tools needed as you work on other projects. All the patterns are marked for construction and assembly convenience. If you are a beginner make a few of these flowers to learn the techniques and gain confidence before moving on to more difficult projects.
If you are a more experienced intarsia artist, use this flower project to experiment with different shaping techniques.

Note the shades of wood shown here are a variation of pattern shades suggested on page 32. To create a variety of flowers, rearrange the placement of dark, medium, and light shades.

No. of pieces 10
Finished size 7½ in x 8¼ in

Wood needed
Light Western red cedar – 14 in x 4 in
Medium Western red cedar – 10 in x 4 in
Dark Western red cedar – 4 in x 4 in

Refer to this project for basic instructions and tools needed as you work on other projects.

1 Enlarge (p15) the pattern on page 33 to the desired size. Make a template of the pattern (p15).

2 Choose ¾-in thick wood, paying attention to grain direction, as marked on pattern.

3 Lay template pieces on the suggested shades of wood and trace onto the wood. Draw the lines of the petals (optional) onto the wood freehand.

Note The grain on the two parts of the leaves runs in the same direction so can be cut out separately or as one piece, cutting the center line later for a good fit between the two leaf halves (p17). Run the saw blade down the join lines holding pieces tight together. This technique requires some practice and a steady hand on the saw.

4 Make sure saw blade is square to the table (p12). With a scroll saw use a #7 PG sharp blade with skip reverse-tooth configuration. If you use a band saw choose a ⅛ in #14 or #15 TPI blade.

5 Cut out pieces carefully on the line.

6 To make a good fitting center, hold the petal template pieces together on the shade of wood suggested (p32), and trace the center space using a sharp pencil and holding the pencil at a 45° angle (p16). Cut out the center piece, cutting on the outside of the line. The piece will be slightly too big, but requires only a little sanding to fit well.

7 Check edges to make sure they are square, especially on the tight corners. Also check bottom edge for tear-out slivers, which can interfere with the fit. The reverse-tooth scroll saw blade will not leave any slivers but the band saw blade will. Sandpaper these off.

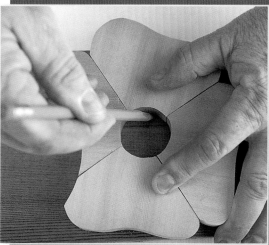

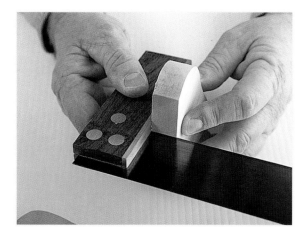

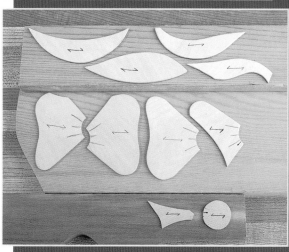

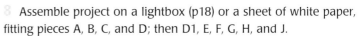

8 Assemble project on a lightbox (p18) or a sheet of white paper, fitting pieces A, B, C, and D; then D1, E, F, G, H, and J.

9 Look down through the joints and mark any high points with a pencil. Sand these down with an oscillating spindle sander (p17).

10 When you start to shape and sand the center, mark the bottom of it and petal at the mid point to get it into the same place each time, as shown below. This is also a good time to cut in the kerf lines on the petals, if desired. Mark first with pencil (see pattern).

11 Continue to assemble the flower and check the fit (left) until you are satisfied. A saw kerf or ¹⁄₁₆-in space between the pieces is acceptable. The shadow created by the shaping disguises the gap quite well. A larger gap between a couple of pieces can often be evened out during the glue-up stage. If you want all the pieces to fit airtight, carry on sanding and checking the fit.

12 Reassemble the project for shaping and sanding. Since the flower is

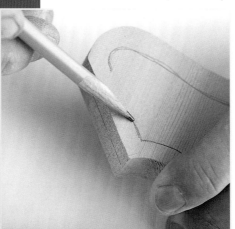

being done in a flat style, all the pieces are the same thickness. The edges in this project are rounded about ³⁄₈ in for a soft look. Mark a piece with reference lines (p21). Use a guide to mark on the reference line, or a marking gauge. A square can also be used to mark the top of a piece and join the lines freehand.

13 Using a small pneumatic sanding drum (p14) and left top (p31), shape all the pieces down to the reference lines, as shown.

14 Reassemble the project and check the shaping. There should be a smooth transition from one piece to another with no flat edges showing.

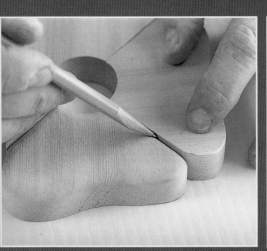

Left Reassemble project for shaping and sanding.
Middle Mark reference line on the top of the piece freehand.
Right A marking gauge shows how far down to round edges.

15 Using a flap sander (p14) sand all the pieces smooth. It isn't necessary to go over 220 grit, which will only create more dust. You

Do not use a router to round over small pieces. It is too dangerous.

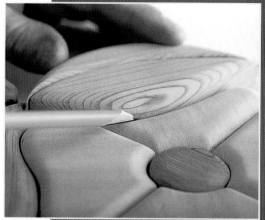

can also sand by hand.

16 For the back, use ¼-in baltic birch plywood. I prefer to cut the back full size and round it back (p23).

17 Assemble the project on the backing material, trace around it and cut out on the line using a scroll or band saw.

18 Assemble the project onto the cut-out back and, using ordinary carpenter's glue, start to glue one piece at a time. Spread glue on the bottom of the piece only, as shown. Place the piece back into the project and adjust the fit. This glue allows 10 to 15 minutes to move the pieces and spread out any gaps among a number of pieces.

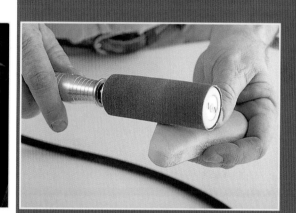

19 When clamping is necessary, as with a long piece near the edge of

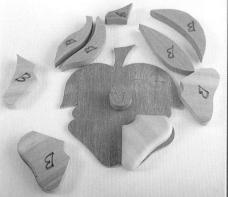

a project or if the backing material is warped, use spring clamps and protect the surface with a scrap piece of plywood (p24).

Note Store the template pieces for each project in a pizza box. If a particular project needs a piece or two clamped, make clamping pads and keep them in the pizza box with the template pieces for next time.

Letters identify pieces of one project when making multiple projects.

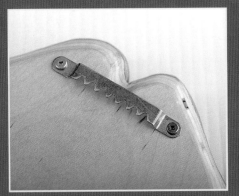

20 Allow the glue to dry for at least 30 minutes, longer if possible. Then round over the back edges with a small pneumatic sander drum (or use a belt sander or a router, but keep your fingers away from the bit).

21 The inside corners can be sanded with a small hard rubber drum, ½-in diameter, as shown. I use mine in a power carver.

22 Finish sanding the back with a flap sander, as shown.

23 The project is now ready for the finish. Apply liquid durathane or varathane with a good brush (p25). Dilute the first coat with 10 percent

thinner, allow to dry, and then sand with 120-grit sandpaper and vacuum it off. Apply the second coat full strength, making sure to wipe the edges with a dry brush (p26) to prevent runs. When the second coat is dry, finish the back by applying the back coat full strength and wipe the edges.

24 When the back coat is dry, sand the front with 220-grit sandpaper and vacuum it off. Then apply the final coat full strength and wipe the edges and allow to dry.

25 To attach the hanger, find the center of the back of project and attach a 2-in sawtooth hanger (p25).

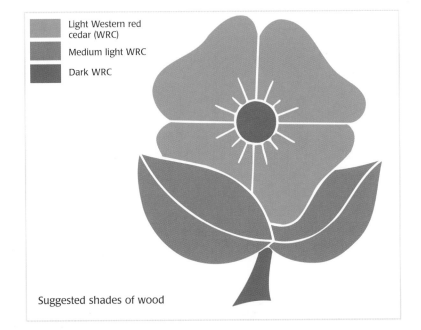

Light Western red cedar (WRC)

Medium light WRC

Dark WRC

Suggested shades of wood

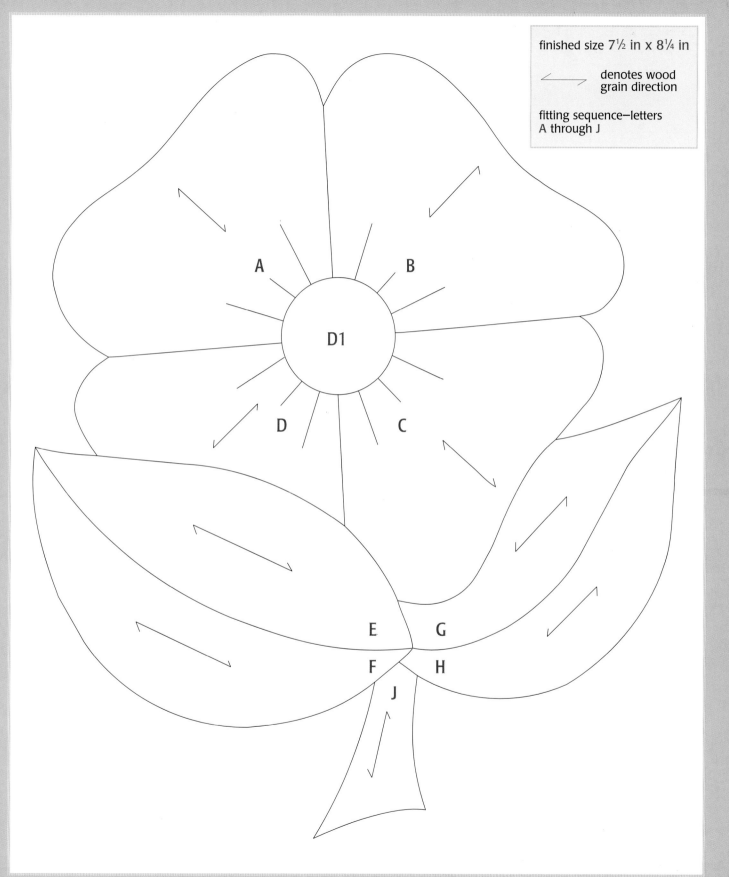

Rose

No. of pieces 28
Finished size 12 in x 19 in

Wood needed
Light Western red cedar − 1 in x 1 in
Medium dark Western red cedar − 6 in x 6 in
Dark Western red cedar − 2 in x 2 in
Aromatic cedar − 6 in x 20 in

1 Enlarge (p15) the pattern on page 36 to the desired size. Make a template (p15) of the pattern.

2 Choose ¾-in thick wood, paying attention to grain direction as marked on pattern.

3 Lay template pieces onto the wood shades or types as pattern suggests, and trace (p15) onto the wood.

4 Use a scroll saw and cut out with a #7 PGT style sharp blade. Make sure blade is square to the table (p12).

5 Cut out pieces carefully on the traced line.

6 Assemble pieces on a lightbox (p18) and check fit. The pieces should fit together as closely as possible but a space (a saw kerf or 1/16 in) between pieces is acceptable.

7 Begin fitting with the center cluster around the heart-shaped center and work outward. A, B, and C; E and D; F; G, H, and I; J, K, and L; then try piece N. If it does not fit, go back and tighten up the cluster. Tape the cluster to a scrap piece of plywood with double-sided tape to hold it together. Either carefully run the scroll saw blade (p17) down between the pieces, or sand the edges lightly with an oscillating spindle sander (p17). Reassemble and try piece N again. Then fit M, O and P, and R and S. Fit remaining pieces, and the stem and leaves.

8 Raise and lower pieces (p19) as the pattern suggests. Pieces O and L, stem, thorn, and small leaf, remain ¾ in thick.

R	raise 1/8 in	L	lower 1/8 in
R1	raise 1/4 in	L1	lower 1/4 in
R2	raise 3/8 in	L2	lower 3/8 in
R3	raise 1/2 in		

9 Reassemble pieces and mark on reference lines (p21). These lines will help with shaping. Shape and round over to these lines.

10 Assemble project on backing material (p23). Trace around it, remove pieces, and cut out the backing (p23). Reassemble project on the cut-out back. This project is ready to glue.

11 Use ordinary white carpenter's glue. Glue up in the same order that it was fitted. It may be necessary to clamp piece A. Use a spring clamp, protecting the surface with a piece of scrap wood (p24). Keep all the pieces of the project on the backing material during glue-up. The glue will allow 10 to 15 minutes to reposition pieces if necessary. Allow to dry.

12 When thoroughly dry, round over the backing edges (p24).

13 Apply the finish (p25). Allow to dry.

14 Attach the hanger (p25).

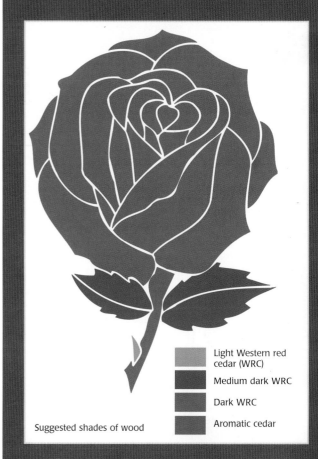

Suggested shades of wood

Light Western red cedar (WRC)

Medium dark WRC

Dark WRC

Aromatic cedar

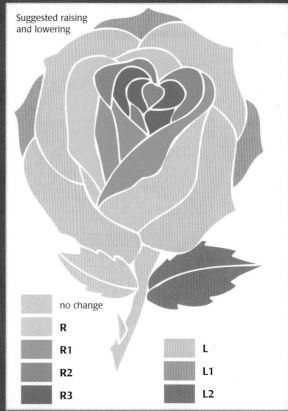

Suggested raising and lowering

no change

R

R1

R2

R3

L

L1

L2

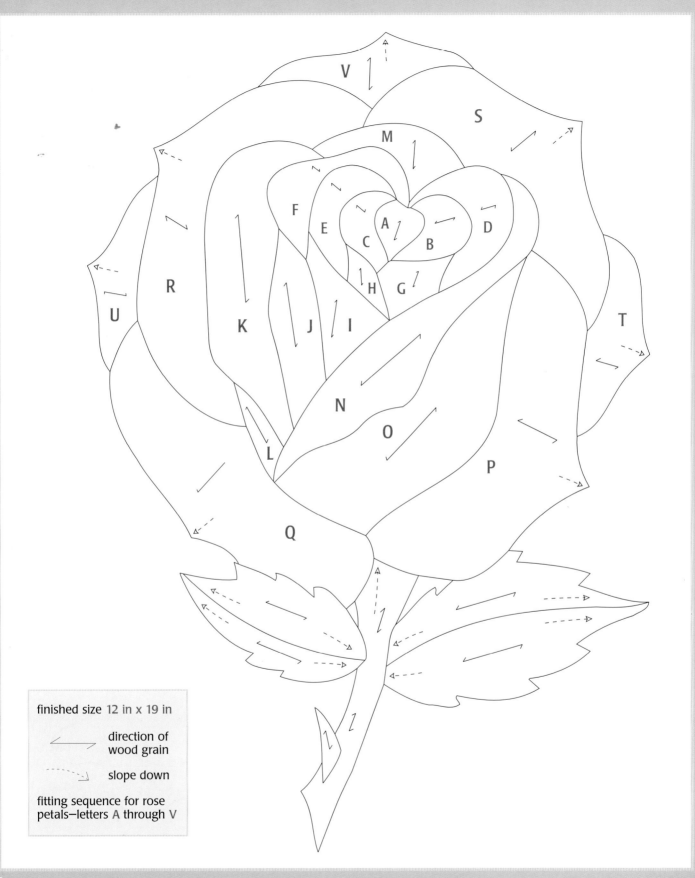

finished size 12 in x 19 in

direction of
wood grain

slope down

fitting sequence for rose
petals—letters A through V

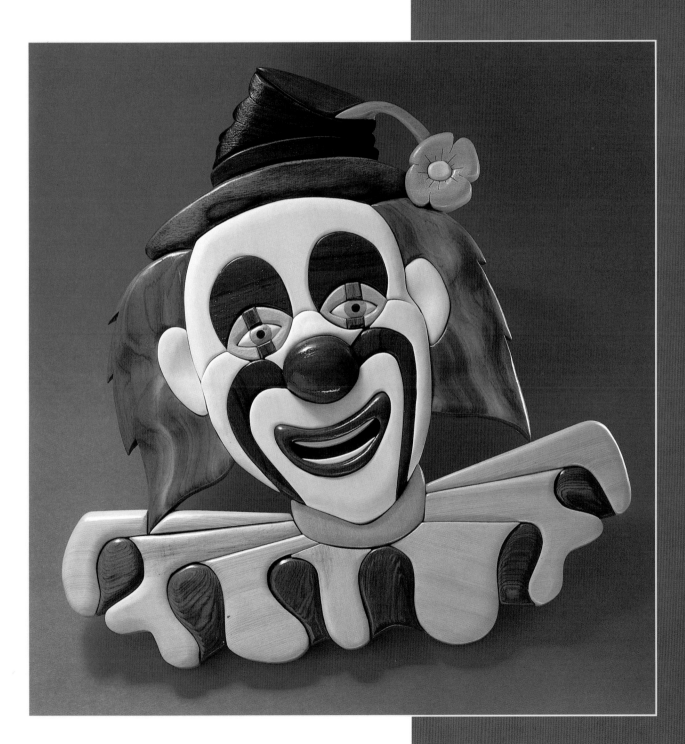

No. of pieces 54
Finished size 17 in x 17 in

Wood needed
Aromatic red cedar (or medium WRC) – 6in x 6 in
Dark Western red cedar – 6 in x 12 in
Paduak (or medium light WRC) – 3 in x 6 in
White aspen (or very light WRC) – 8 in x 16 in
Black walnut (or very dark WRC) – 5 in x 10 in
Green-cast American poplar (or light WRC) –
    2 in x 4 in
Yellow cedar (or pine or spruce) – 6 in x 20 in
Yellow pau amarillo (or pine, or spruce) –
    6 in x 6 in
Red bloodwood (or medium WRC) – 6 in x 6 in
Note   Choose two different shades of light,
medium light, and very light, to give some
contrast. The same with medium and medium
dark. Different grain patterns also offer contrast.

1   Enlarge (p15) the pattern on page 40 to the desired size. Make a template (p15) of the pattern.

2   Choose ¾-in thick wood, paying attention to grain directions as marked on pattern.

3   Lay template pieces onto the wood shades or types as pattern suggests, and trace (p15) onto the wood.

4   Use a scroll saw and cut out with a #7 PGT style sharp blade. Make sure blade is square to the table (p12).

5   Cut out pieces carefully on the traced line. Make eyes, mouth, and flower (p39).

6   Assemble pieces on a lightbox (p18) and check fit. Pieces should fit together as closely as possible but a space (a saw kerf or ¹/₁₆ in) between pieces is acceptable. Fit eye parts in A and B together and fit into C. Fit D to J, then mouth parts into J. Fit ears L and K into hair M and N and fit hair into face. Fit collar O. Fit ruffle from 1 to 14 and hat from 1 to 5. Fit center into flower and fit flower to hair and hat.

7   Raise and lower pieces (p19) as pattern suggests.

R	raise ⅛ in	L1	lower ¼ in
R1	raise ¼ in	L2	lower ⅜ in
R3	raise ½ in	L4	lower ⅝ in

8   Reassemble pieces and mark on reference lines (p21). These lines will help with shaping. Shape and round over to these lines.

9   Assemble project on backing material (p23). Trace around it, remove pieces, and cut out the backing (p24). Reassemble project on the cut-out back. Project is ready to glue.

10   Use ordinary white carpenter's glue. Glue up in the same order that it was fitted. It may be necessary to clamp piece A. Use a spring

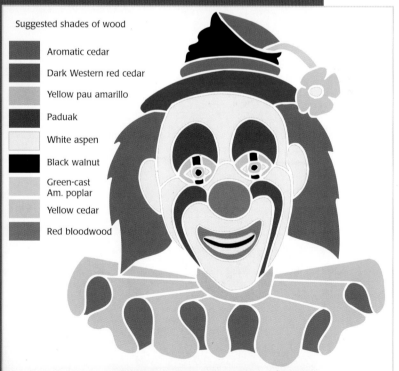

Suggested shades of wood

- Aromatic cedar
- Dark Western red cedar
- Yellow pau amarillo
- Paduak
- White aspen
- Black walnut
- Green-cast Am. poplar
- Yellow cedar
- Red bloodwood

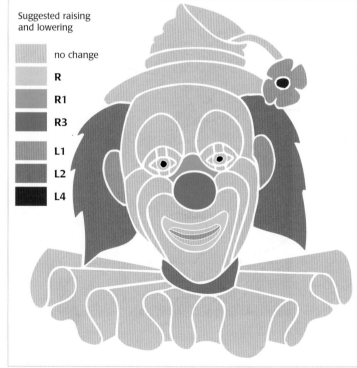

Suggested raising and lowering

- no change
- R
- R1
- R3
- L1
- L2
- L4

clamp, protect the surface with a piece of scrap wood. Keep all pieces of project on backing material during glue-up. The glue will allow 10 to 15 minutes to reposition pieces, if necessary. Allow to dry.

11 When thoroughly dry, round over the backing edges (p24).

12 Apply the finish (p25). Allow to dry.

13 Attach the hanger (p25).

Making clown eyes

 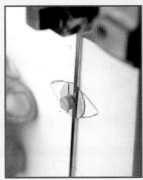 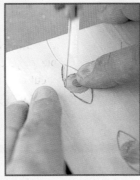  

1 Trace eyes onto 1½ in x 4 in white aspen. Drill out ⅝ in centers, ½ in deep.

2 Use green wood dowel cut with ⅝-in tenon cutter. Make dowels ¾ in long. Glue in holes leaving ⅛ in protruding. Dry for 30 minutes.

3 Drill ¼ in holes, ⅜ in deep, into green dowels (place in center or to one side).

4 Insert and glue in ¼ in black walnut dowels, ½ in long.

5 Make glint in clown's eyes with ⅛ in holes in black walnut, ¼ in deep, to insert ⅛ in dowel, ⅜ in long.

6 When all dowels are inserted and glue is dry, turn block of white wood on its side and trim all dowels flush with scroll or band saw.

7 Finally, cut out eyes and shape them.

Making clown mouth

1 Cut out entire mouth from part J.

2 Trace mouth hole onto red wood to make lips. Cut this piece out inside line. Sand to fit. Cut out center part of lips.

3 Trace hole in center of lips onto white aspen for teeth. Optional—Make teeth with kerf marks (p79).

4 Cut out dark wood piece for mouth opening between teeth and fit in place.

Making flower for hat

1 Cut out flower, then cut out center.

2 Trace center onto white aspen, cut out on outside of line, leaving line.

3 Sand to fit.

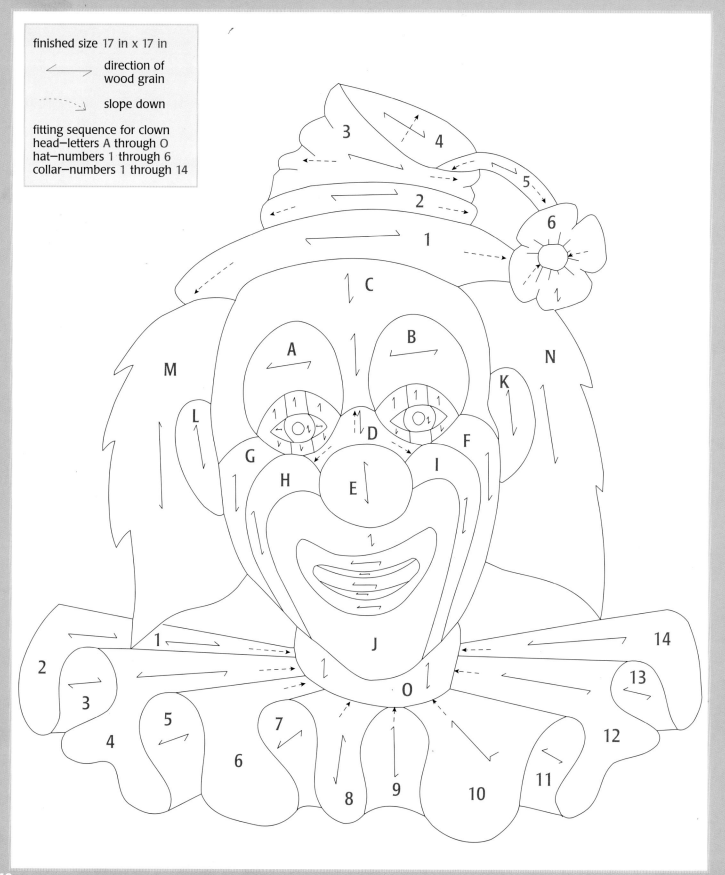

finished size 17 in x 17 in

→ direction of wood grain

⇢ slope down

fitting sequence for clown head—letters A through O hat—numbers 1 through 6 collar—numbers 1 through 14

Ying Yang

No. of pieces 35
Finished size 18½ in x 14½ in

Wood needed
Light Western red cedar − 2 in x 8 in
Medium light Western red cedar − 2 in x 5 in
Dark light Western red cedar − 1 in x 4 in
Medium Western red cedar − 5 in x 8 in
Medium dark Western red cedar − 4 in x 9 in
Dark Western red cedar − 8 in x 30 in
White aspen (or pine or spruce) − 6 in x 8 in
Black walnut (or very dark cedar) − 7 in x 18 in

1 Enlarge (p15) the pattern on page 43 to desired size. Make a template (p15) of the pattern.

2 Choose ¾-in thick wood, paying attention to grain directions as marked on pattern.

3 Lay template pieces onto the wood shades or types as pattern suggests, and trace (p15) onto the wood.

4 Use a scroll saw and cut out with a #7 PGT style sharp blade. Make sure blade is square to the table (p12).

5 Cut out pieces carefully on the traced lines.

6 Assemble pieces on a lightbox (p18) and check fit. Pieces should fit together as closely as possible, but a space (a saw kerf or ¹⁄₁₆ in) between pieces is acceptable.

7 Begin fitting from A in order through to R, then fit mountain #1 and fit into place. Then mountain #2 and fit into place. Fit part 3 into 4 and part 5 into 6. Fit 4 and 6 together. Finally fit the ying yang into place between the mountains and the tree.

8 Raise and lower pieces (p19) as the pattern suggests.

R	raise ⅛ in	L	lower ⅛ in
R1	raise ¼ in	L1	lower ¼ in
		L2	lower ⅜ in

Check for any rough edges, slivers, or high points and sand, as needed.

9 Reassemble and mark on reference lines (p21). These lines will help with shaping. Shape and round over to these lines. Shape the tree round to the outside edges, also the mountains. The outside edges of the ying yang should be well rounded, but the center line only slightly rounded.

10 Assemble project on the backing material (p23). Trace around it, remove the pieces, and cut out the backing (p23). Reassemble project on the cut-out back and project is ready to glue.

11 Use ordinary white carpenter's glue. Glue this project in the same order as the fitting, above. Some of the longer parts (A,G,K) may need to be clamped. Use spring clamps and protect the wood surface with a scrap piece of wood (p24). Make sure all the project pieces stay on the backing material during glue-up. Carpenter's

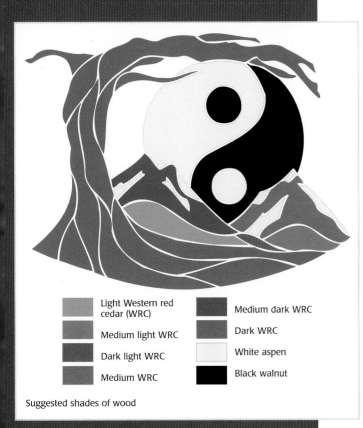

Suggested shades of wood

Light Western red cedar (WRC)	Medium dark WRC
Medium light WRC	Dark WRC
Dark light WRC	White aspen
Medium WRC	Black walnut

Suggested raising and lowering

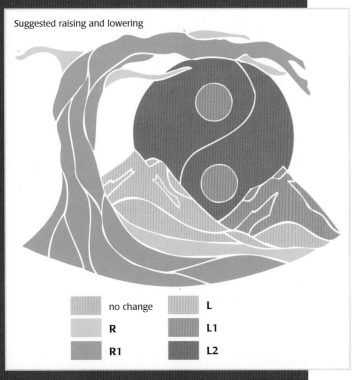

no change	L
R	L1
R1	L2

glue will allow 10 to 15 minutes to reposition a piece, if necessary. Allow to dry.

12 Round over the backing edges (p24).

13 Apply a durathane semi-gloss finish (p25).

14 Attach the hanger (p25).

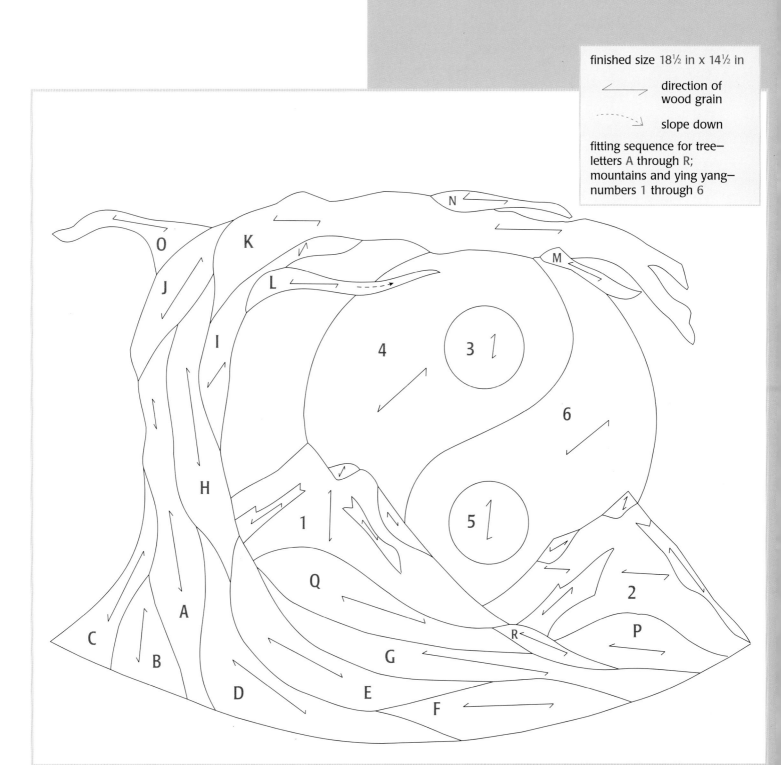

finished size 18½ in x 14½ in

direction of wood grain

slope down

fitting sequence for tree— letters A through R; mountains and ying yang— numbers 1 through 6

No. of pieces 19
Finished size 16½ in x 5½ in

Wood needed
Light Western red cedar – 12 in x 3 in
Medium Western red cedar – 12 in x 5½ in
Dark Western red cedar – 14 in x 5½ in
White aspen (or holly or spruce) – 1 in x 1 in
Black walnut (or very dark cedar) – 1 in x 1 in

1   Enlarge (p15) the pattern on page 46 to the desired size. Make a template (p15) of the pattern.

2   Choose ¾-in thick wood, paying attention to grain directions as marked on pattern.

3   Lay template pieces onto the wood shades or types as pattern suggests, and trace (p15) onto the wood.

4   Use a scroll saw and cut out with a #7 PGT style sharp blade. Make sure blade is square to the table (p12).

5   Cut out pieces carefully on the traced line. Make eyes. Cut out eye pieces. They are small so use #3 double-tooth blade and slow saw to 900 SPM. Fit carefully.

6   Assemble pieces on a lightbox (p18) and check fit. The pieces should fit together as closely as possible, but a space (a saw kerf or ¹⁄₁₆ in) between pieces is acceptable.

7   This project is fairly easy to fit. Begin with A and fit in order through to Q. Fit eye.

8   Raise and lower pieces (p19) as the pattern suggests.
    R   raised ⅛ in   L2 lower ⅜ in
    R1 raised ¼ in
Check for rough edges, slivers, or high points and sand as needed.

9   Reassemble and mark on reference lines (p21) These lines will help with the shaping. Shape and round to these lines to give fish body a round realistic shape. For easier shaping, temporarily glue body pieces (p22) to a piece of scrap wood and shape them as one piece. Remove pieces from scrap wood. Mark fins, gil, and tail lines with a pencil and burn with a wood burning tool (p15).

10   Assemble project on backing material (p23). Trace around it, remove the pieces, and cut out the back (p23). Reassemble pieces on the cut-out back and project is ready to glue.

11   Use ordinary white carpenter's glue. Glue up this project in the same order as the fitting above. The long parts (A,B,C) may need to be clamped. Use a spring clamp, and protect the wood surface with a scrap piece of wood (p24). Allow to dry for 30 minutes, remove clamps, and continue the glue-up.

12   Keep all project pieces on backing material during glue-up. Carpenter's glue will allow 10 to 15 minutes to reposition pieces, if necessary. Allow to dry.

13   Round over the backing edges (p24).

14   Apply the finish (p25).

15   Attach the hanger (p25).

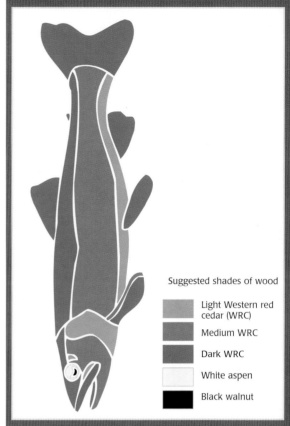

Suggested shades of wood

Light Western red cedar (WRC)

Medium WRC

Dark WRC

White aspen

Black walnut

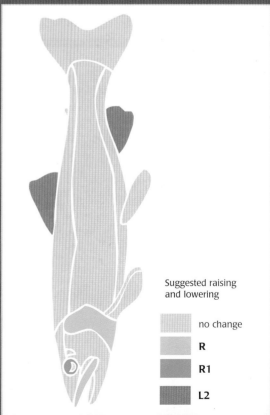

Suggested raising and lowering

no change

R

R1

L2

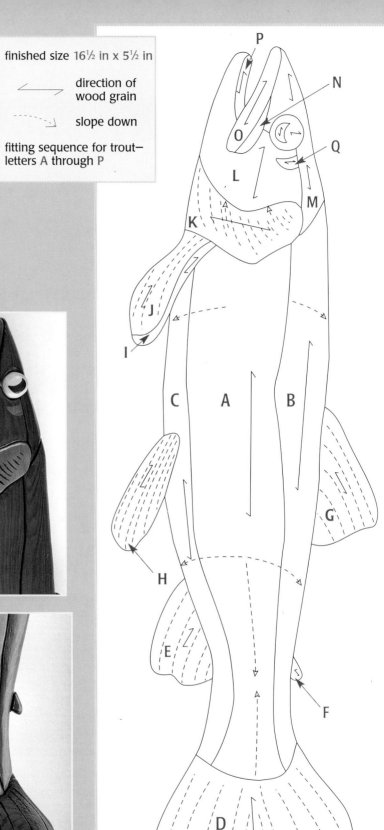

finished size 16½ in x 5½ in

→ direction of wood grain

⇢ slope down

fitting sequence for trout—letters A through P

The dotted lines indicated on pattern are burned on the gil, fins, and tail with a wood burning tool.

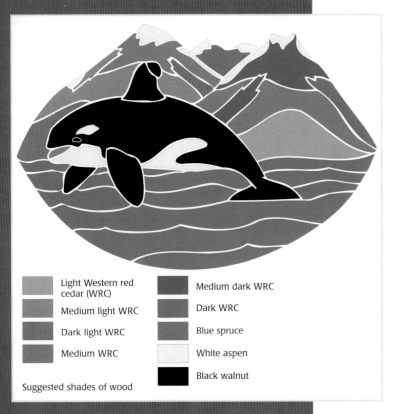

Light Western red cedar (WRC)

Medium light WRC

Dark light WRC

Medium WRC

Medium dark WRC

Dark WRC

Blue spruce

White aspen

Black walnut

Suggested shades of wood

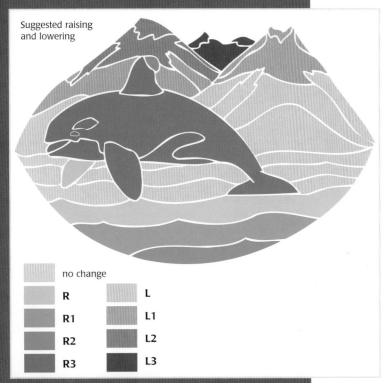

Suggested raising and lowering

no change

R

R1

R2

R3

L

L1

L2

L3

No. of pieces 45
Finished size 19 in x 13 in

Wood needed
Light Western red cedar − 2 in x 8 in
Medium light Western red cedar − 2 in x 5 in
Dark light Western red cedar − 1 in x 4 in
Medium Western red cedar − 5 in x 8 in
Medium dark Western red cedar − 4 in x 9 in
Dark Western red cedar − 8 in x 30 in
Blue spruce (find boards with a blue-gray marking on the wood,
    or coarse-grained light WRC or spruce) − 16 in x 24 in
White aspen (or pine or spruce) − 6 in x 8 in
Black walnut (or very dark cedar) − 7 in x 18 in

1   Enlarge (p15) the pattern on page 49 to the desired size.
Make a template (p15) of the pattern.
2   Choose ¾-in thick wood, paying attention to grain
directions as marked on pattern.
3   Lay template pieces onto the wood shades or types as
pattern suggests, and trace (p15) onto the wood.
4   Use a scroll saw and cut out with a #7 PGT style sharp
blade. Make sure blade is square to the table (p12).
5   Cut out pieces carefully on the traced line. Make eye by
drilling a ⅜ in hole where marked, ½ in deep. Sand end of ⅜
in black walnut dowel cut ⁹⁄₁₆ in long. Insert and glue in piece
R. Piece V is an inside cut. Cut it out, place piece U on white
wood and trace hole. Cut out inside the line. Sand as needed
and fit in place.
6   Assemble pieces on a lightbox (p18) and check fit. The
pieces should fit together as closely as possible but a space (a
saw kerf or ¹⁄₁₆ in) between pieces is acceptable. Fit in order A
through W, then numbers 1, 2, then mountains pieces 3
through 11, then M1 to M4, and finally 12 through 16.
7   Raise and lower pieces (p19) as the pattern suggests.

R	raise ⅛ in	L	lower ⅛ in
R1	raise ¼ in	L1	lower ¼ in
R2	raise ⅜ in	L2	lower ⅜ in
R3	raise ½ in	L3	lower ½ in

8   Reassemble pieces and mark on reference lines (p21).
These lines will help with shaping. Shape and round over to
these lines.
9   Assemble project on backing material (p23). Trace around
it, remove the pieces, and cut out backing (p23). Reassemble
project on the cut-out back. Project is ready to glue.
10   Use ordinary white carpenter's glue. Glue up in the same
order that it was fitted. It may be necessary to clamp piece A.
Use a spring clamp, protect the surface with a piece of scrap
wood (p24).

Keep all pieces of the project on backing material during glue-up. Carpenter's glue will allow 10 to 15 minutes to reposition pieces, if necessary. Allow to dry.

11 When thoroughly dry, round over the backing edges (p24).

12 Apply the finish (p25). Allow to dry.

13 Attach the hanger (p25).

Samples of BSP choices of wood:
Left spruce *Middle* coarse-grained light WRC *Right* blue spruce

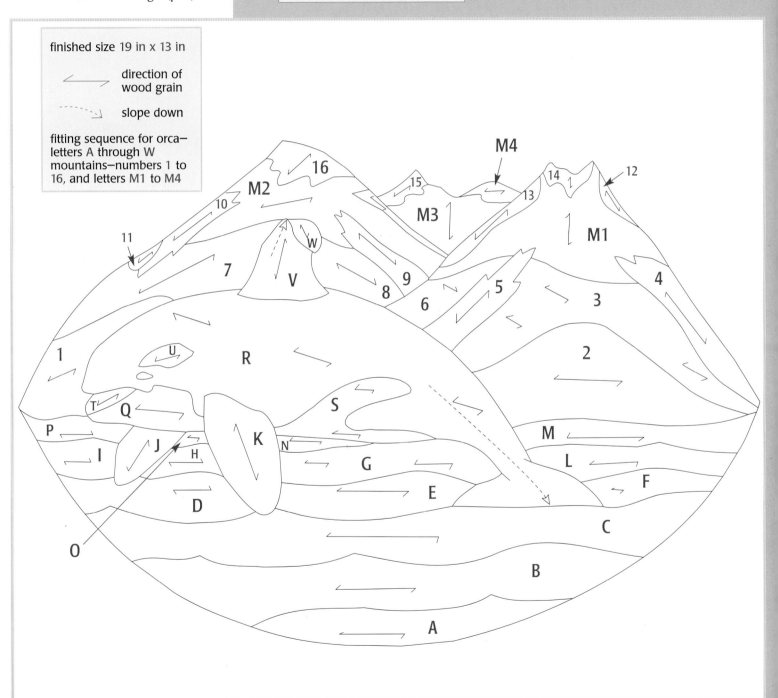

finished size 19 in x 13 in

direction of wood grain

slope down

fitting sequence for orca—letters A through W mountains—numbers 1 to 16, and letters M1 to M4

Dolphins

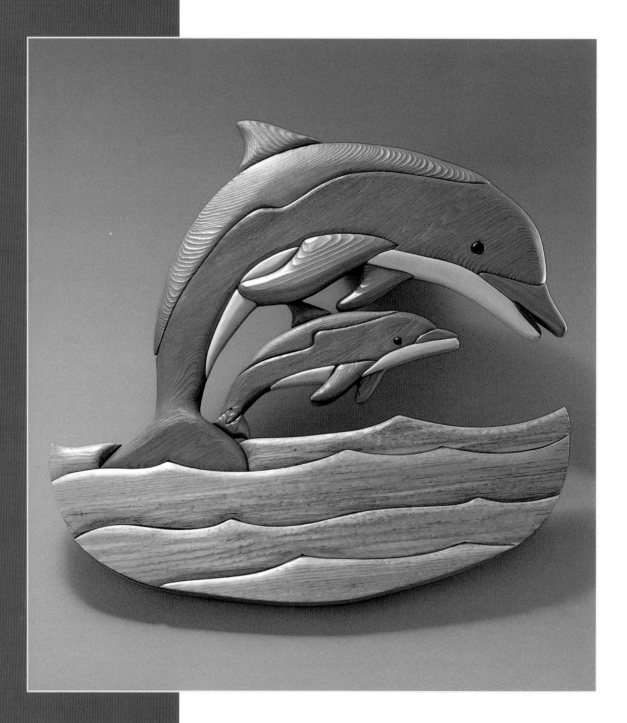

No. of pieces 23
Finished size 16 in x 15 in

Wood needed
Light Western red cedar (WRC) − 6 in x 14 in
Medium light WRC − 8 in x 16 in
Aromatic red cedar − 1 in x 1½ in
Blue spruce (find boards with a blue-gray marking on the wood)
    or coarse-grained light WRC or spruce − 16 in x 24 in
White aspen, pine, or spruce − 3 in x 8 in

1   Enlarge (p15) the pattern on page 52 to the desired size. Make a template (p15) of the pattern.

2   Choose ¾ in thick wood, paying attention to grain directions as marked on pattern.

3   Lay template pieces onto the wood shades or types as the pattern suggests, and trace onto the wood (p15).

4   This project is all softwood. Use a scroll saw and cut out with a #5 or #7 PGT style sharp blade. Make sure the blade is square to the table (p12).

5   Cut out the pieces carefully on the traced lines. Make eye for mother by drilling ⅜ in hole where marked ½ in deep. Insert ⅜ in black walnut dowel ⁹⁄₁₆ in long. Round top. Glue in. For baby, drill ¼ in hole ⅜ in deep. Insert ¼ in black walnut dowel ⁹⁄₁₆ in long. Round top. Glue in.

6   Assemble pieces on a lightbox (p18) and check fit. The pieces should fit together as closely as possible, but a space (a saw kerf or ¹⁄₁₆ in) between pieces is acceptable. First fit water piece A, then B and C. Fit F into C, E, and D; G to F; H to G; M to F; L to F; and I to F. Then fit J, K, N, and O.

7   Then fit the small dolphin beginning with 9 to 1; 2 to 1; 3 to 2; 4 to 1; 5 to 1 and 7; 7 and 6; 8 to 7 and 1.

8   Use a ⅜ in drill press and drill the eye holes ½ in deep for the large dolphin and ¼ in deep for the small dolphin. Round the end of a ⅜ in black walnut dowel with sandpaper and cut a piece ⁹⁄₁₆ in. This will allow the eye to stick out a bit from the eyehole of the dolphin when the eye is inserted. Use a dab of carpenter's glue in the bottom of the hole. Repeat the procedure for the small eye but cut it ⁷⁄₁₆ in long and insert the same as with the large dolphin.

9   Raise and lower pieces (p19) as the pattern suggests.

R	raise ⅛ in	L	lower ⅛ in
R1	raise ¼ in	L1	lower ¼ in
		L2	lower ⅜ in

10   Reassemble pieces and mark on reference lines (p21). Shape and round over to these lines. Shape the tail down to the water so it appears to be coming out of the water.

11   Apply gel finish before glue-up.

12   Assemble project on backing (p23). Trace around it and cut out (p23). Reassemble on the cut-out back using method 1 (p23). The project is ready to glue.

13   Use ordinary white carpenter's glue and begin with water pieces A, B, and C. Because of their length they may need to be clamped. Use

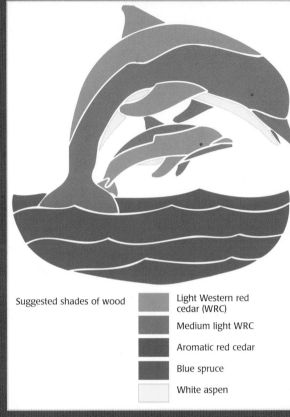

Suggested shades of wood

	Light Western red cedar (WRC)
	Medium light WRC
	Aromatic red cedar
	Blue spruce
	White aspen

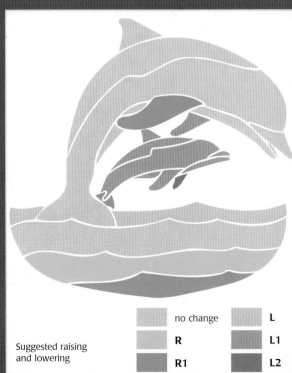

Suggested raising and lowering

	no change		L
	R		L1
	R1		L2

Make dolphin eyes using drill press and dowels.

spring clamps and protect the surface with a piece of scrap wood. Allow to dry for 30 minutes. Then proceed to glue F, which also may need to be clamped. Then glue in pieces D and E; G; and H, M, L, I, J, K, O. Glue small dolphin pieces 9, 1, 2, 3, 4, 5, 7, 6, and 8.

13 Keep all the project pieces on the backing material during glue-up. Carpenter's glue will allow 10 to 15 minutes to reposition a piece, if necessary. Allow to dry.

14 Round over the backing edges (p24).

15 Apply a satin gel finish (p25).

16 Attach hanger (p25).

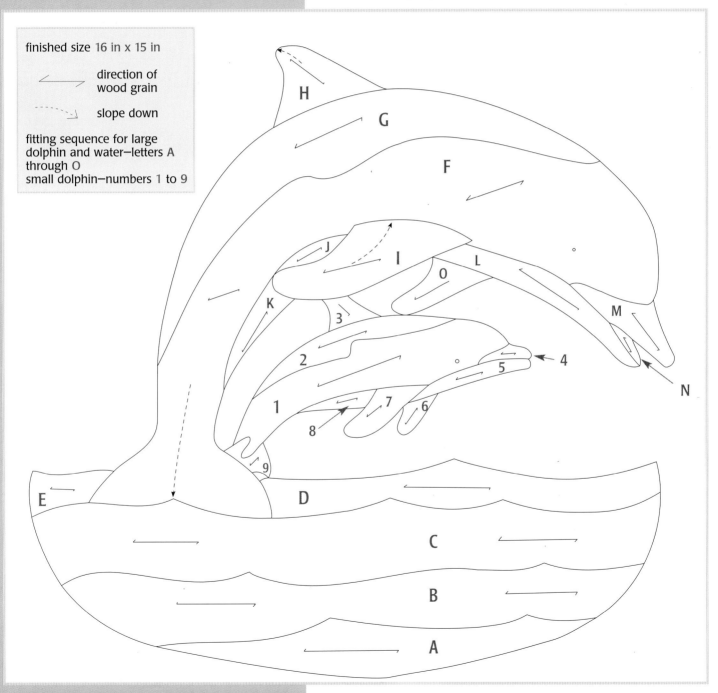

finished size 16 in x 15 in

→ direction of wood grain

⇢ slope down

fitting sequence for large dolphin and water—letters A through O
small dolphin—numbers 1 to 9

Kangaroo

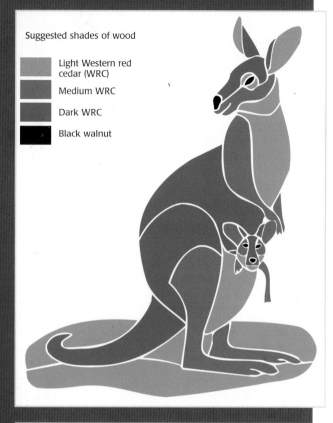

Suggested shades of wood

- ▨ Light Western red cedar (WRC)
- ▨ Medium WRC
- ▨ Dark WRC
- ■ Black walnut

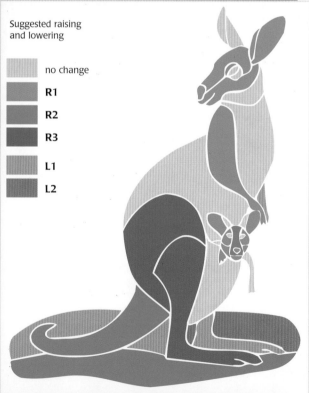

Suggested raising and lowering

- ▨ no change
- ▨ R1
- ▨ R2
- ▨ R3
- ▨ L1
- ▨ L2

No. of pieces 38
Finished size 14½ in x 18 in

Wood needed
Light Western red cedar − 20 in x 5½ in
Medium Western red cedar − 12 in x 5½ in
Dark Western red cedar −18 in x 5½ in
Black walnut or very dark cedar − 1 in x 1 in

1 Enlarge (p15) the pattern on page 55 to the desired size. Make a template (p15) of the pattern.

2 Choose ¾-in thick wood, paying attention to grain directions as marked on pattern.

3 Lay template pieces onto the wood shades or types as pattern suggests, and trace (p15) onto the wood.

4 Use a scroll saw and cut out with a #7 PGT style sharp blade. Make sure blade is square to the table (p12).

5 Cut out the pieces carefully on the traced line. Cut eye pieces W, X, Y, and fit together. Make baby's eye where marked with a wood burning tool (p15).

6 Assemble pieces on a lightbox (p18) and check fit. The pieces should fit together as closely as possible but a space (a saw kerf or ¹⁄₁₆ in) between pieces is acceptable. Begin fitting from the bottom up, from A in order through to I, then K to V. Then fit in the mother kangaroo eye, then fit the pouch J with baby kangaroo.

7 Raise and lower pieces (p19) as the pattern suggests.

R1	raised ¼ in	L1	lower ¼ in
R2	raised ⅜ in	L2	lower ⅜ in
R3	raised ½ in		

8 Reassemble pieces and mark on reference lines (p21). These lines will help with the shaping. Shape and round over to these lines. Slope the baby's nose to the forehead to give more dimension.

9 Assemble project on backing material (p23). Trace around it, remove the pieces, and cut out backing (p23). Reassemble project on the cut-out back. Project is ready to glue.

10 Use ordinary white carpenter's glue. Glue up in the same order that it was fitted. It may be necessary to clamp piece A to other pieces. Use a spring clamp but protect the surface with a piece of scrap wood (p24). Keep all the pieces of the project on the backing material during glue-up. Carpenter's glue will allow 10 to 15 minutes to reposition pieces, if necessary. Allow to dry.

11 When thoroughly dry, round over the backing edges (p24).

12 Apply the finish (p25). Allow to dry.

13 Attach the hanger (p25).

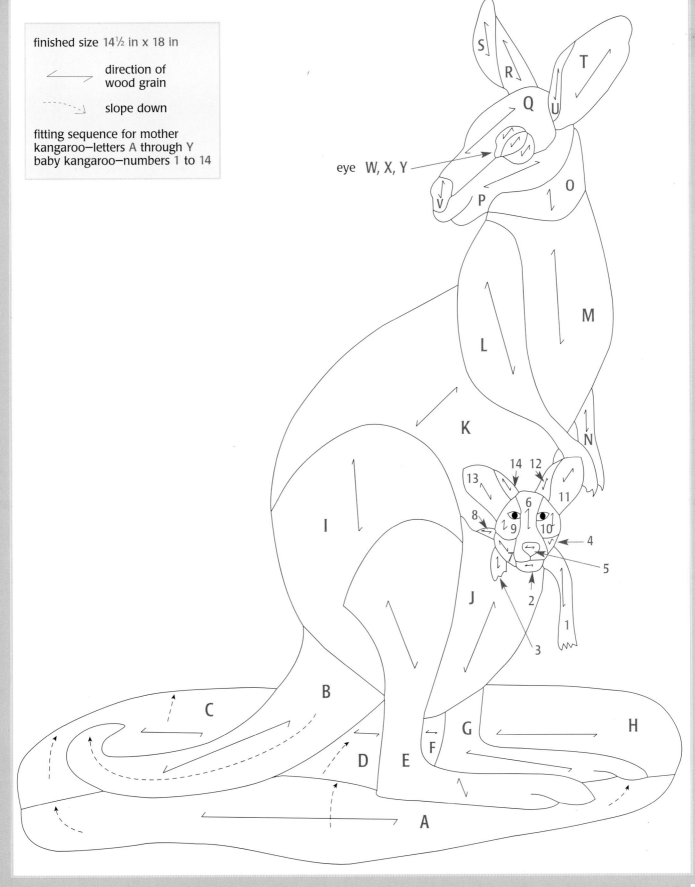

finished size 14½ in x 18 in

direction of wood grain

slope down

fitting sequence for mother kangaroo—letters A through Y
baby kangaroo—numbers 1 to 14

eye W, X, Y

Eagle

No. of pieces 27
Finished size 11 in x 11 in

Wood needed
White aspen (pine or spruce) − 6 in x 20 in
Black walnut (or very dark WRC) − 1 in x 1 in
Wenge (or black walnut or very dark WRC) − 6 in x 10 in
Yellow pau amarillo (or yellow cedar or osaga orange) − 4 in x 4 in

1   Enlarge (p15) the pattern on page 58 to the desired size. Make a template (p15) of the pattern.

2   Choose ¾-in thick wood, paying attention to grain directions marked on pattern.

3   Lay template pieces onto the wood shades or type as pattern suggests, and trace (p15) onto the wood.

4   Use a scroll saw and cut out with a #7 PGT style sharp blade. Make sure blade is square to the table (p12).

5   Cut out pieces carefully on the traced line.

6   Assemble pieces on a lightbox (p18) and check fit. The pieces should fit as closely as possible but a space (a saw kerf or ¹⁄₁₆ in) between pieces is a very good fit. The most difficult pieces to fit in this project are the zigzag lines where A and B meet. This is a good place to begin because once these pieces are in place the others fit more easily. Begin fitting A to B; then B to C; D to C; K to C and D; and E to D; and S to E. Then fit P, Q, and R; then F, G, H, I, J and L. Fit beak pieces M, N, and O together; then fit beak in place. Once pieces are fitted, mark any high points or rough edges and sand as needed.

7   To make the eye, trace the circle of eye pattern part onto white wood (p58). Drill a ¼ in hole for eye pupil and insert a piece of ¼ in wenge or black walnut dowel. Then cut eye out and fit it in place (p58).

8   The feather pieces should be done next. Fit 2 to 3; 4 to 2; and 1 to A and 2 and 3. Fit the rest of feather 5 to 6; 7 to 6; and finally 8 to 7. The completed feather should fit easily to the eagle head.

9   Raise and lower (p19) pieces as the pattern suggests
    R   raise ⅛ in   L   lower ⅛ in
    R2   raise ⅜ in
Check for any rough edges, slivers, or high points and sand where needed.

10   Reassemble the project and mark on the reference lines (p21). These lines will help with the shaping. Shape and round over to these lines (p21). Shape the head to give a realistic look. Shape the beak down to the head, as arrows indicate. At this time draw line on beak piece N and burn in with a wood burning tool (p15).

11   Assemble project on backing material (p23). Trace around it and cut out the back (p23). Reassemble on the cut-out back. The project is ready to glue.

12   Use ordinary white carpenter's glue or an ordinary white glue. Begin to glue this project with the feather and work up from there in the same order as the fitting. If backing material remains flat, no clamping should be necessary. Keep all project pieces on the backing material during glue-up. Carpenter's glue will allow 10 to 15 minutes to

Suggested shades of wood

White aspen

Black walnut

Wenge

Yellow pau amarillo

Suggested raising and lowering

no change

R

R2

L

reposition a piece, if necessary. Allow to dry.

13 Round over the backing edges (p24).

14 Apply the finish (p25). B and Y parts have satin durathane finish, eye has high gloss finish, white parts have latex finish to preserve white color of wood. Allow to dry completely.

15 Attach the hanger (p25).

Making eagle eye

1 Trace outside eye pattern on wood (p57).
2 Drill hole (p57).
3 Round one end of dowel and Insert.
4 Cut out eye with scroll saw.
5 Remove eye plug and place in project as instructed.

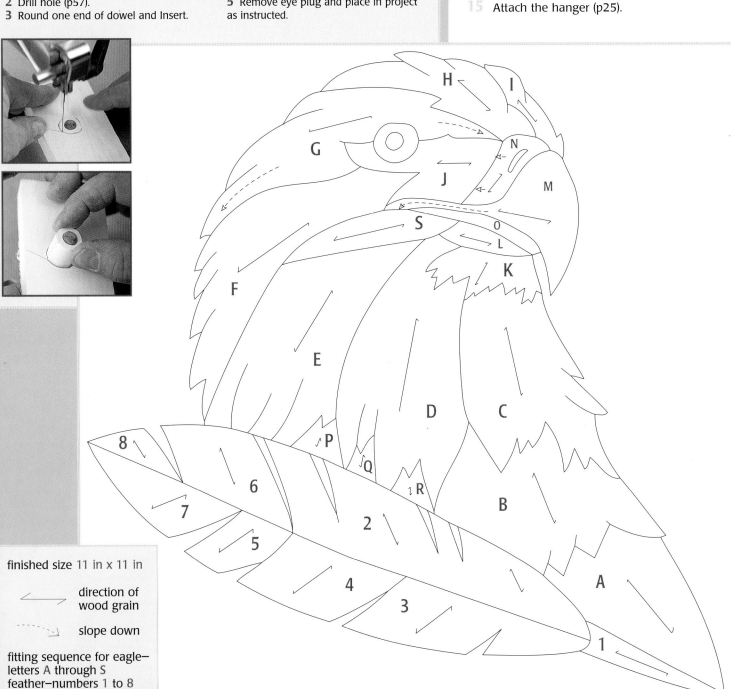

finished size 11 in x 11 in

— direction of wood grain

-- slope down

fitting sequence for eagle—
letters A through S
feather—numbers 1 to 8

Pumpkin

Suggested shades of wood

	Light Western red cedar (WRC)
	Medium light WRC
	Medium WRC
	Dark WRC
	Black walnut
	Yellow pau amarillo

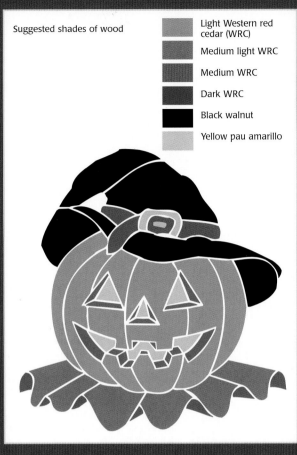

Suggested raising and lowering

	L			no change
	L1			R
				R1
				R2
				R3

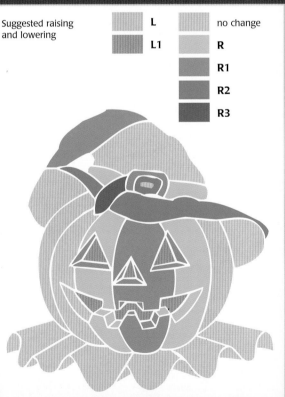

No. of pieces 58
Finished size 16 in x 17 in

Wood needed

Light Western red cedar – 6 in x 30 in
Medium light Western red cedar – 6 in x 12 in
Medium Western red cedar – 6 in x 6 in
Dark Western red cedar – 6 in x 6 in
Black walnut (or very dark cedar) – 6 in x 18 in
Yellow pau amarillo (or osage–orange or satin) – 6 in x 6 in

1 Enlarge (p15) the pattern on page 61 to the desired size. Make a template (p15) of the pattern.

2 Choose ¾-in thick wood, paying attention to grain directions as marked on pattern.

3 Lay template pieces onto the wood shades or types as pattern suggests, and trace (p15) onto the wood.

4 Use a scroll saw and cut out with a #7 PGT style sharp blade. Make sure blade is square to the table (p12).

5 Cut out pieces carefully on the traced line. Cut out piece in center of buckle separately.

6 Assemble pieces on a lightbox (p18) and check fit. The pieces should fit together as closely as possible but a space (a saw kerf or ¹/₁₆ in) between pieces is acceptable. The small triangle pieces in eyes and nose are fitted with larger yellow triangles, and sloped down to yellow pieces. The small pieces of the mouth are sloped to the yellow lower pieces.

7 Begin fitting pumpkin parts A through F. Then fit in eye, nose, and mouth parts. Then the ruffle starting with G through S, in order. Fit hat part 1 to the pumpkin, then fit in order 2, 3, and 4 into 5; and 6. Then fit 7 and 8; 9 and 10; and 11.

8 Raise and lower pieces (p19) as the pattern suggests.

R	raised ⅛ in	L	lower ⅛ in
R1	raised ¼ in	L1	lower ¼ in
R2	raised ⅜ in		
R3	raised ½ in		

Check for rough edges, slivers, or high points and sand smooth.

9 Reassemble pieces and mark on reference lines (p21). These lines will help with the shaping. Shape and round over to these lines. Shape to give the pumpkin a rounded look. Shape the small pieces inside the mouth, eyes, and nose down to the yellow wood.

10 Assemble project on backing material (p23). Trace around it, remove pieces, and cut out the backing (p23). Reassemble pieces on the cut-out back and project is ready to glue.

11 Use ordinary white carpenter's glue. Glue this project in the same order as the fitting above. Parts A and F, and part 1 may need to be clamped. Use spring clamps and protect the wood surface with a piece of scrap wood (p24). Make sure all project pieces stay on the backing material during glue-up. Carpenter's glue will allow 10 to 15 minutes to reposition a piece, if necessary. Allow to dry.

12 Round over the backing edges (p24).

13 Apply a satin gel finish (p25). Allow to dry completely.

14 Attach the hanger (p25).

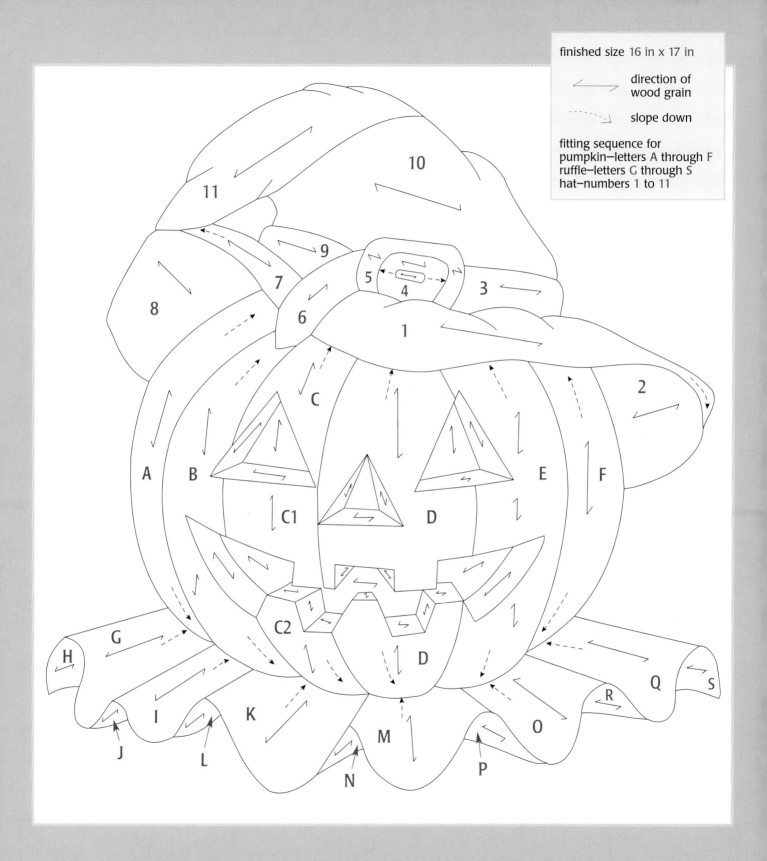

finished size 16 in x 17 in

direction of wood grain

slope down

fitting sequence for
pumpkin–letters A through F
ruffle–letters G through S
hat–numbers 1 to 11

Candy Canes

No. of pieces 35
Finished size 11 in x 14 in

Wood needed
Light Western red cedar − 4 in x 4 in
Medium Western red cedar − 3 in x 4 in
Dark cedar − 4 in x 4 in
Aromatic red cedar − 6 in x 12 in
White aspen (or pine or spruce) − 6 in x 10 in
Red bloodwood (or stain a light wood) − 2 in x 5 in

1   Enlarge (p15) the pattern on page 64 to the desired size. Make a template (p15) of the pattern.

2   Choose ¾-in thick wood, paying attention to grain directions as marked on pattern.

3   Lay template pieces onto wood shades or types as pattern suggests and trace (p15) onto the wood.

4   Use a scroll saw and cut out with a #7 PGT style sharp blade. Make sure blade is square to the table (p12).

5   Cut out pieces carefully on the traced line. Mark pattern pieces on the corresponding wood piece as you cut them out. This will be helpful as you fit and reassemble the project.

6   Assemble pieces on a lightbox (p18) and check fit. The pieces should fit as closely as possible but a space (a saw kerf or 1/16 in) is acceptable. Mark any rough edges, slivers, or high points and sand smooth. Lines on leaves are inside scroll cuts. Mark on lines, drill small hole, disconnect blade, thread through hole, reconnect, and cut out.

7   Fit holly berries together, then the leaves. Begin fitting candy cane pieces from the center out (A, B, C in order through to Y). Finally fit the two ribbons. Make any adjustments necessary.

8   Raise and lower pieces (p19) as pattern suggests.

R	raised ⅛ in	L	lower ⅛ in
R1	raised ¼ in	L2	lower ⅜ in
R2	raised ⅜ in		

9   Reassemble pieces and mark on reference lines (p21). These lines will help with shaping. Shape berries round to the surrounding pieces, and slightly round over the edges of the leaves. The candy canes should have a rounded look and the sides of the ribbons should also be rounded.

10   Assemble project on the backing material. Trace around it, remove pieces and cut out (p23). Reassemble on cut-out backing and prepare to glue (p23). Use backing method 1 (p23).

11   Use ordinary white carpenter's glue. Glue pieces in the same order that the pieces were fit onto the lightbox. If the backing material is flat clamping any pieces should not be necessary. Keep all project pieces on the backing material during glue-up. Carpenter's glue dries slowly and you will have 10 to 15 minutes to reposition pieces for the best fit. Allow to dry.

12   Round over the backing edges (p24).

13   Apply a satin gel finish (p25). Dry completely.

14   Attach the hanger (p25).

Suggested shades of wood

	Light Western red cedar (WRC)		Aromatic cedar
	Medium dark WRC		White aspen
	Dark WRC		Red bloodwood

Suggested raising and lowering

	no change		
	R		
	R1		L
	R2		L2

finished size 11 in x 14 in

↙——→ direction of
wood grain

⌐⌐⌐↘ slope down

fitting sequence for candy
canes—letters A through Y

Mare and Colt

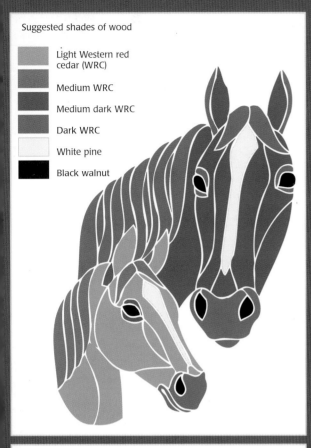

Suggested shades of wood

Light Western red cedar (WRC)

Medium WRC

Medium dark WRC

Dark WRC

White pine

Black walnut

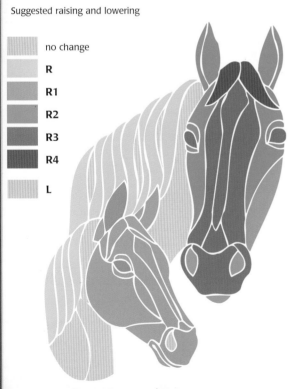

Suggested raising and lowering

no change

R

R1

R2

R3

R4

L

No. of pieces 62
Finished size 22 in x 16 in

Wood needed
Light Western red cedar − 20 in x 5½ in
Medium Western red cedar − 7 in x 5½ in
Medium dark Western red cedar − 28 in x 5½ in
Dark Western red cedar − 30 in x 5½ in
White pine (or Mississippi maple or spruce or holly) − 10 in x 3 in
Black walnut (or very dark cedar) − 6 in x 3 in

1 Enlarge (p15) the pattern on page 67 to the desired size. Make a template (p15) of the pattern.

2 Choose ¾-in thick wood, paying attention to grain directions as marked on pattern.

3 Lay template pieces onto the wood shades or types as pattern suggests, and trace (p15) onto the wood.

4 Use a scroll saw and cut out with a #7 PGT style sharp blade. Make sure blade is square to the table (p12).

5 Cut out pieces carefully on the traced line.

6 Assemble pieces on a lightbox (p18) and check fit. The pieces should fit together as closely as possible, but a space (a saw kerf or ¹⁄₁₆ in) between pieces is acceptable. This project is challenging to fit. Begin with mare head from A in order through to O. Fit in eyes and nostrils, then P, and then the mane parts beginning with 1 in order through to 11. Now fit colt in order from A through to P. Fit in eye and nostril, then the mane in order from 1 through to 5, and finally fit Q and R.

7 Raise and lower pieces (p19) as pattern suggests. Raise pieces in this project with ¼ in oak plywood. Check for any slivers, rough edges, or high points and sand smooth.

R	raise	⅛ in	L	lower	⅛ in
R1	raise	¼ in			
R2	raise	⅜ in			
R3	raise	½ in			
R4	raise	⅝ in			

8 Reassemble pieces and mark on reference lines (p21). These lines will help with shaping. Shape and round over to these lines.

9 Assemble project pieces on backing material (p23). Use ⅜ in thick baltic birch for this project. Trace around it, remove pieces, and cut out the backing (p23). Reassemble project on the cut-out back and project is ready to glue.

10 Use ordinary white carpenter's glue. Glue up in the same order as pieces were fitted above. Keep all project pieces on the backing material during glue-up. Carpenter's glue will allow 10 to 15 minutes to reposition a piece, if necessary, to achieve the best fit.

11 When thoroughly dry, round over the backing edges (p24).

12 Apply the finish (p25). Allow to dry.

13 Attach the hanger (p25).

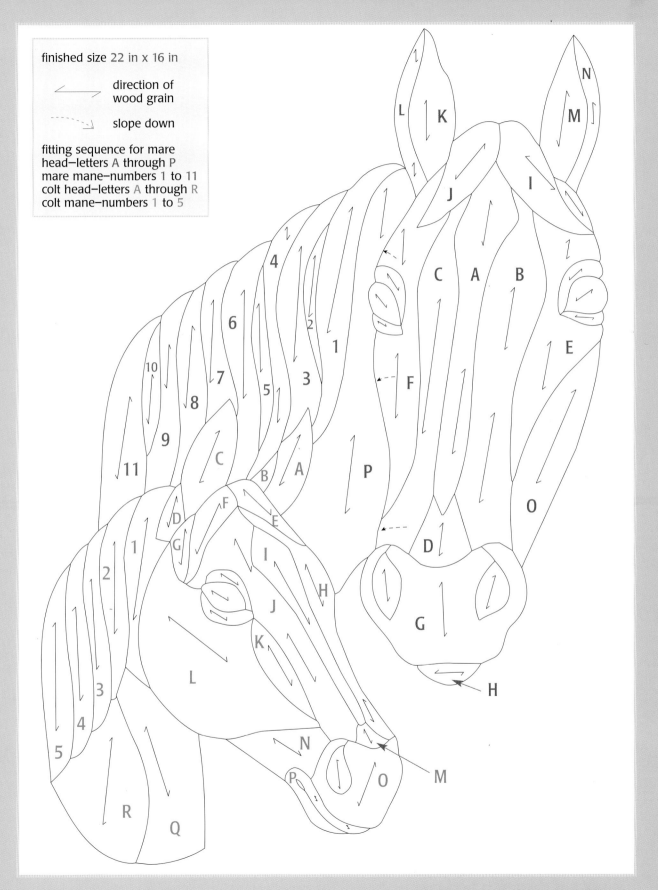

finished size 22 in x 16 in

direction of
wood grain

slope down

fitting sequence for mare
head—letters A through P
mare mane—numbers 1 to 11
colt head—letters A through R
colt mane—numbers 1 to 5

No. of pieces 41
Finished size 17½ in x 16 in

Wood needed
Light cedar — 20 in x 5½ in
Medium cedar — 8 in x 3 in
Medium dark cedar — 8 in x 4 in
Dark cedar — 4 in x 4 in
White pine (or Mississippi maple or spruce or holly) — 16 in x 5½ in
Black walnut (or very dark cedar) — 8 in x 4 in
for bullets
⅜ in dowels (ordinary white dowels, usually birch) ¾ in length
Black walnut (or stain), ¾ in length

1   Enlarge (p15) the pattern on page 71 to the desired size. Make a template (p15) of the pattern.

2   Choose ¾-in thick wood, paying attention to grain direction as marked on pattern.

3   Lay template pieces onto the wood shades or types as pattern suggests, and trace onto the wood (p15).

4   Use a scroll saw and cut out with a #7 PGT style sharp blade. Make sure blade is square to the table (p12).

5   Cut out pieces carefully on the traced line. Make bullets, and gun (p70).

6   Assemble pieces on a lightbox (p18) and check fit. The pieces should fit together as closely as possible, but a space (a saw kerf or ¹⁄₁₆ in) between pieces is very good. For this project, fit boots first from A through F, then O. The gun and hat can be fitted separately, and then fitted onto the boots. Fit hat from 1 to 4. Drill ½ in holes in hat band ½ in deep. Round end of ½ in black walnut dowels or medium cedar ⁷⁄₁₆ in long and fit in holes. Glue into piece 3. Then fit holster from Z1 to Z to W. Then fit Q to P and both to W. Then S1 into S and R, onto V and U, finally fit T. Fit gun.

7   Make bullets, as shown. Glue end to end, then shape end. Glue bullets on belt where indicated.

8   Make gun barrel. Drill ⅜ in hole in end, as shown on page 70.

9   Make gun cylinder. Carve out marked areas with small drum sander, as shown on page 70. Add stitch marks on holster with wood burning tool (p15).

10   Raise and lower project pieces (p19) as pattern suggests. Raised areas marked with R have an additional ¼ in oak plywood. Check for any rough edges, slivers, or high points and sand smooth.

R	raise	⅛ in	L	lower	⅛ in
R1	raise	¼ in	L2	lower	¼ in
R2	raise	⅜ in			

11   Reassemble pieces and mark on reference lines (p21). These lines will help with shaping. Shape and round over to the lines shown. Use ½ in dowel for holes in hat and.

12   Assemble project on the backing material (p23). Trace around it, remove pieces, and cut out the backing (p23). Reassemble on the cut-

Making bullets

1 Glue two shades of doweling together end to end. Use black walnut and ordinary white dowel. If using one shade of doweling, coat half with a dark stain. Allow to dry.

2 When dry, check size against pattern piece. Trim to size.

3 Using a small pneumatic drum sander, shape bullets at dark end. Sand one side of the bullet slightly flat for more gluing surface. Glue in place where pattern indicates.

4 Detail of bullets glued in place.

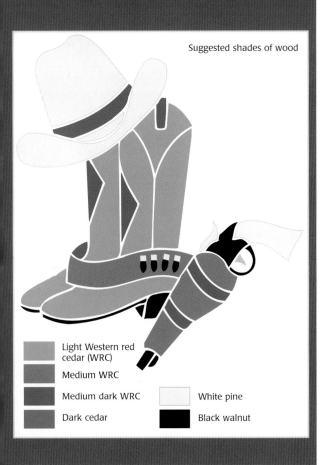

Suggested shades of wood

Light Western red cedar (WRC)	
Medium WRC	
Medium dark WRC	White pine
Dark cedar	Black walnut

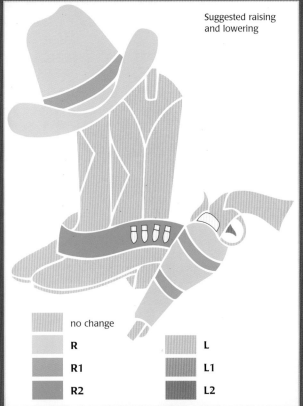

Suggested raising and lowering

	no change		
	R		L
	R1		L1
	R2		L2

out back. Prepare to glue.

13 Use ordinary white carpenter's glue. Glue up in the same order indicated above for fitting. This project may require clamping, especially for pieces 1, A, B, and D. Use a spring clamp, and protect wood surface with a piece of scrap (p24) wood. Keep all project pieces on the backing material during glue-up. The glue will allow 10 to 15 minutes to reposition a piece, if necessary. Allow to dry.

14 Round over the backing edges (p24).

15 Apply the finish (p25). Allow to dry.

16 Attach the hanger (p25).

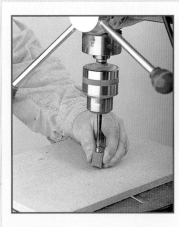

Making gun barrel

1 Cut out pattern pieces P and Q. Using a drill press or hand drill, drill ⅜ in hole in end of pattern piece P.

2 Sand barrel side flat to give barrel an octagon shape.

Making gun cylinder

1 Mark carved areas on gun cylinder pattern piece.

2 Carve out with small pneumatic drum sander. Glue cylinder to backing material.

3 Fit cylinder into gun pieces R and S. Fit pieces T, U, V. Fit gun to holster pieces.

4 Detail of finished cylinder.

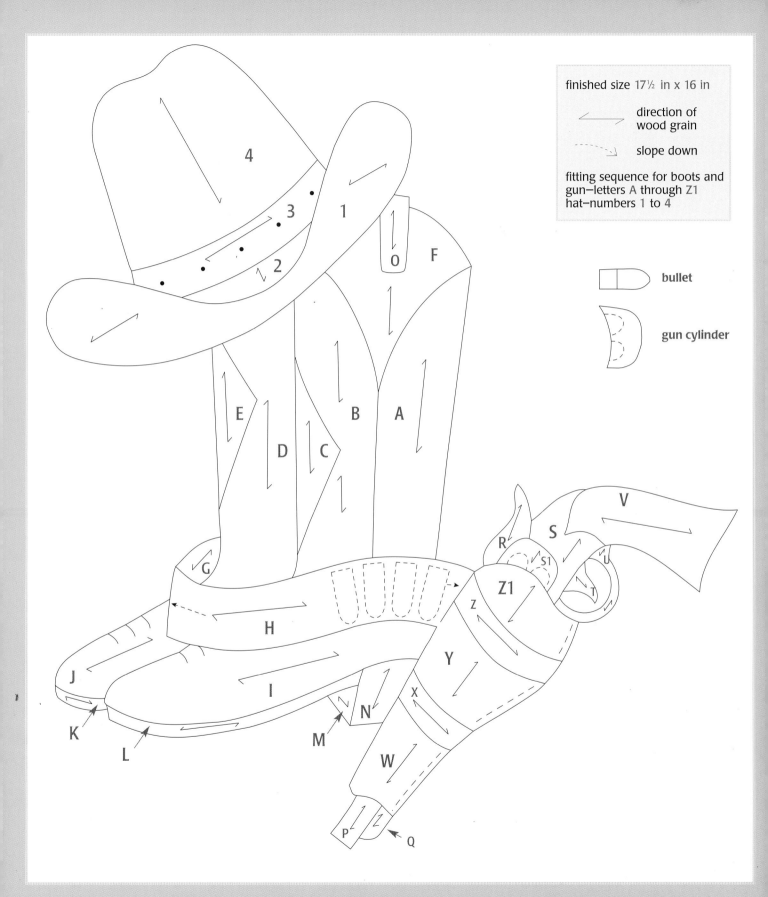

finished size 17½ in x 16 in

direction of wood grain

slope down

fitting sequence for boots and gun—letters A through Z1 hat—numbers 1 to 4

bullet

gun cylinder

Blue Jay and Trillium

No. of pieces 73
Finished size 15 in x 13½ in

Wood needed
Medium Western red cedar — 10 in x 5½ in
Medium dark Western redcedar — 6 in x 5½ in
Dark Western redcedar — 6 in x 5½ in
White aspen (or Mississippi maple or pine or holly) — 10 in x 5½ in
Black walnut (or very dark cedar) — 4 in x 1 in
Green-cast American poplar (or sumac or a light cedar) — 9 in x 5½ in
Sumac — 4 in x 2 in
Yellow cedar — 1 in x 1 in

1 Enlarge (p15) the pattern on page 74 to the desired size. Make a template (p15) of the pattern.

2 Choose ¾-in thick wood, paying attention to grain directions marked on pattern.

3 Lay template pieces onto the wood shades or types as pattern suggests, and trace (p15) onto the wood.

4 Use a scroll saw and cut out with a #7 PGT style sharp blade. Make sure blade is square to the table (p12).

5 Cut out pieces carefully on the traced line. To cut out single feathers, see page 74. Make eye. Hold pieces A and B tightly together and drill ⅜ in hole, ½ in deep, as indicated on pattern. Use a drill press to make hole straight. Cut ⅜ in dowel ⁹⁄₁₆ in long, round one end. Glue in hole.

6 Assemble pieces on a lightbox (p18) and check fit. The pieces should fit together as closely as possible, but a space (a saw kerf or ¹⁄₁₆ in) between pieces is acceptable. Begin fitting with blue jay pieces A in order through to Q, then fit wing 1 though 19, then fit and place wing pieces and R. Fit T, S, U, and tree stump pieces 1 to 5, then fit tree stump small pieces 6 to 8; then fit and place cluster #1 starting at A then B, C, D, then E, F, and finally G1 and 2, H1 and 2, and J1 and 2. Then cluster #2 starting with center A, then B, C, D, then E, F, and finally G1 and 2, J1 and 2, and H1 and 2. Mark any high points and sand smooth.

7 Raise and lower pieces (p19) as pattern suggests.

    R   raised ⅛ in   L   lower ⅛ in
    R2 raised ¼ in
    R3 raised ³⁄₁₆ in

Raised areas marked with R have an additional ¼ in oak plywood.

8 Reassemble pieces and mark on reference lines (p21). Shape and round over to these lines. Round bird body, leaves, and stump.

9 Assemble project on the backing material (p23). Trace around it, remove pieces, and cut out the backing (p23). Reassemble project on the cut-out back. The project is ready to glue.

10 Use ordinary white carpenter's glue and glue up in the same order that is given above for fitting the pieces. Keep backing material flat so that clamping will not be necessary. Keep all project pieces on the backing material during glue-up. Carpenter's glue dries slowly so you will have 10 to 15 minutes to reposition pieces.

11 When thoroughly dry, round over the backing edges (p24).

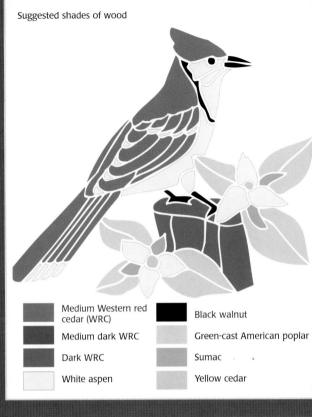

Suggested shades of wood

	Medium Western red cedar (WRC)		Black walnut
	Medium dark WRC		Green-cast American poplar
	Dark WRC		Sumac
	White aspen		Yellow cedar

Suggested raising and lowering

	no change		
	R		L
	R2		
	R3		

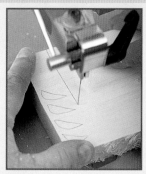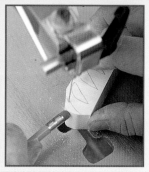

Cutting single feathers

1 Trace pattern for individual feathers onto selected wood.

2 Using scroll saw, make first cut. Then use eraser end of a pencil to hold the piece while making the last cut.

12 Apply the finish (p25). Allow to dry.

13 Attach the hanger (p25).

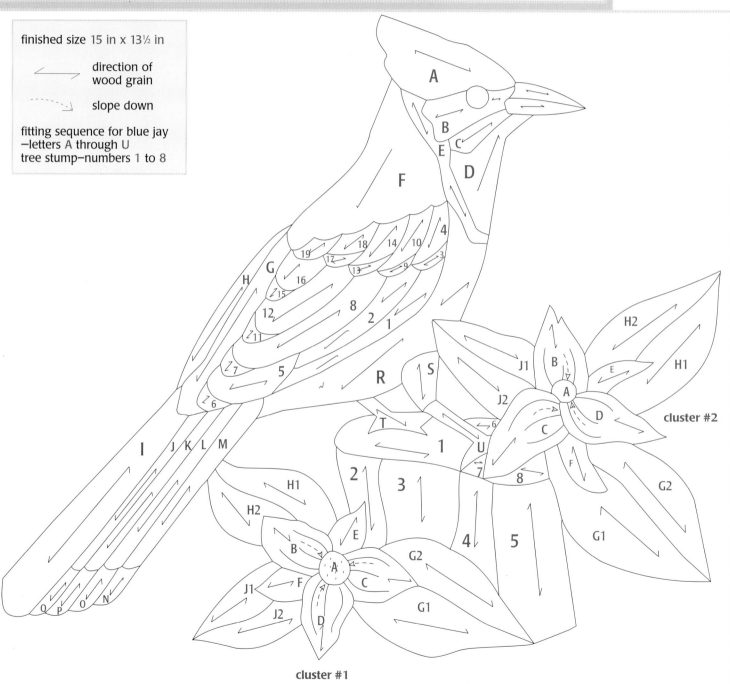

finished size 15 in x 13½ in

direction of wood grain

slope down

fitting sequence for blue jay
—letters A through U
tree stump—numbers 1 to 8

A

B

C

E

D

F

G

H

18 14 10
19 17   4
16   13 9   3
Z15
12   8   2   1
Z11
Z7   5
Z6

I J K L M

Q P O N

cluster #2

H2

H1

J1 B E
A
J2   D
C
6
F
U
7
8
G2

S
R
T
1
2
3
4 5 G1

H1
H2
E
B
A
J1 F C
J2   G2
D
G1

cluster #1

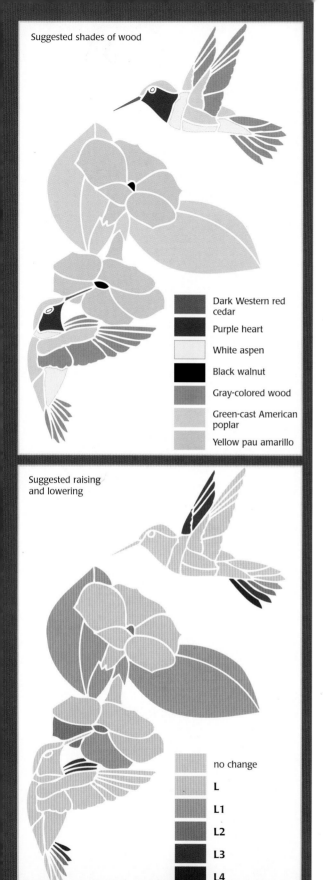

Suggested shades of wood

▨	Dark Western red cedar
▰	Purple heart
▱	White aspen
■	Black walnut
▨	Gray-colored wood
▤	Green-cast American poplar
▤	Yellow pau amarillo

Suggested raising and lowering

▱	no change
▨	L
▨	L1
▨	L2
▰	L3
■	L4

No. of pieces 27 (single bird) / 48 (flower and bird)
Finished size 7½ in x 6 in (single bird) / 11 in x 9 in (flower and bird)

Wood needed
Dark Western red cedar − 1 in x 2 in
Purple heart (or medium dark WRC) − 2 in x 4 in
White aspen (or holly or light WRC) − 4 in x 6 in
Black walnut (or very dark WRC) − 1 in x 1 in
Gray-colored wood such as red gum (or light WRC) − 6 in x 8 in
    (or spruce boards sometimes have gray/blue areas)
Green-cast American poplar (or medium WRC) − 6 in x 12 in
Yellow pau amarillo (or yellow cedar or spruce or pine) − 6 in x 8 in

1 Enlarge (p15) the pattern on page 77 to the desired size. Make a template (p15) of the pattern.

2 Choose ¾-in thick wood, paying attention to grain directions as marked on pattern.

3 Lay template pieces onto the wood shades or types as pattern suggests, and trace (p15) onto the wood.

4 This project uses pau amarillo for the yellow color which is a very hard wood subject to burning. Use a scroll saw and cut with a #9 PGT style sharp blade or a band saw with a ⅛ in blade 14 or 15 TPI. Other woods can be cut with a #7 PGT style sharp blade. Make sure blade is square to the table (p12).

5 Cut pieces out carefully on the traced line. Make eye in parts A in both birds. Drill ¼ in holes, ⅜ in deep in A before you cut out. Insert a piece of ¼-in black walnut dowel ⁷⁄₁₆ in long. Then cut out part A. Lines on larger wing parts are kerf lines to represent feathers. Trace them across selected wood, then cut kerf lines one at a time holding onto the bigger piece of wood (see p79).

6 Assemble pieces on a lightbox (p18) and check fit. Pieces should fit as closely as possible, but a space (a saw kerf or ¹⁄₁₆ in) between pieces is acceptable. Fitting will be easier if you begin with the single bird. Start from A to B; C, E, D; then F. Fit wings separately and then fit them to the body. Next fit G; then the tail feathers starting with J in order to P. (See cutting single feathers on page 74.) Finally fit beak. Remaining pieces are a little more challenging to fit. Fit bird in the same way as the single bird. Then begin to fit flower pieces in order 1 through 5. Fit center. Fit A and B to the flower; H to I; G to F; then both sets to the flower. Leave flower pieces C, D, and E. Proceed with flower pieces 6 through 10, fit center, and fit to parts G and H. Fit bird into flower − 6 through 10

7 Raise and lower pieces (p19) as pattern suggests.

L	lower ⅛ in	L3	lower ½ in
L1	lower ¼ in	L4	lower ⅝ in
L2	lower ⅜ in		

Center of flower is L2. Slope petals down to center. Check pieces for any rough edges, slivers, or high points and sand smooth.

8 Reassemble pieces and mark on reference lines (p21). These lines will help with shaping. Shape and round over to these lines on all pieces. Shape petals of the flowers down to the center and round

leaves down to each end. Shape and round over the birds to give them a realistic look.

9   Assemble each project on the backing material (p23). Trace around them and cut out the backing (p23). Reassemble projects on the cut-out backing and they are ready to glue.

10   Use ordinary white carpenter's glue. Glue this project in the same order indicated above for fitting. If backing material is flat, pieces should not need clamping. Keep all project pieces on backing material during glue-up. Carpenter's glue will allow 10 to 15 minutes to reposition a piece, if necessary. Allow to dry.

11   Round over the backing edges (p24)

12   Apply a durathane satin finish (p25). Allow to dry.

13   Attach the hanger (p25).

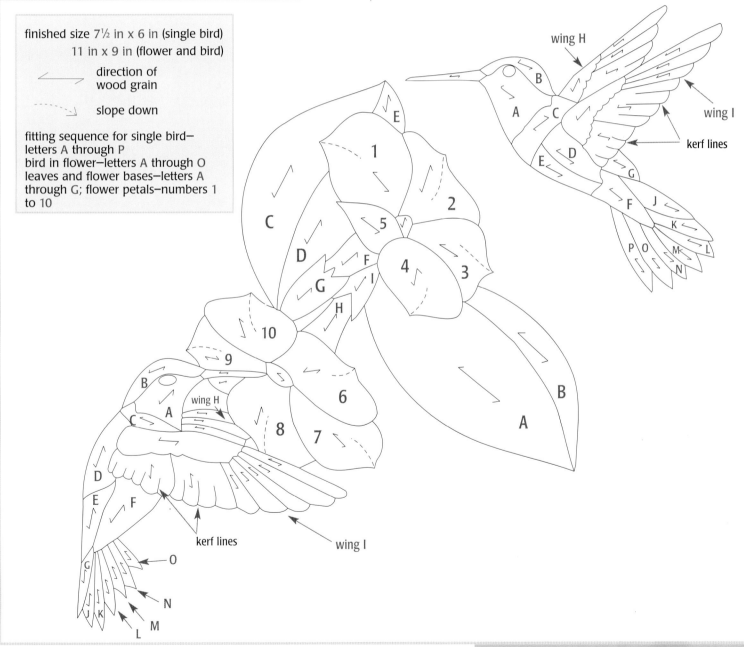

finished size 7½ in x 6 in (single bird)
         11 in x 9 in (flower and bird)

⟶   direction of wood grain

⇢   slope down

fitting sequence for single bird—
letters A through P
bird in flower—letters A through O
leaves and flower bases—letters A
through G; flower petals—numbers 1
to 10

Touring Motorcycle

No. of pieces 74
Finished size 21 in x 12½ in

Wood needed
Aromatic red cedar — 10 in x 5½ in
Pine — 9 in x 4 in
White spruce (or Mississippi maple or basswood) — 16 in x 5½ in
Black walnut (or very dark cedar) — 6 in x 5½ in
Yellow cedar (or yellow colored pine) — 9 in x 5½ in

1 Enlarge (p15) the pattern on page 80 to the desired size. Make a template (p15) of the pattern.

2 Choose ¾-in thick wood, paying attention to grain directions marked on pattern.

3 Lay template pieces onto the wood shades or types as pattern suggests, and trace (p15) onto the wood.

4 Use a scroll saw and cut out with a #7 PGT style sharp blade. Make sure blade is square to the table (p12).

5 Cut out pieces carefully on the traced line. The center of the air-breather cover Part A is not a separate piece. Drill ¾ in hole ¼ in deep to represent circle. Part F is a ¾ in dowel ¹⁄₁₆ in longer than hole depth and rounded off.

6 Assemble pieces on a lightbox (p18) and check fit. Pieces should fit as closely as possible but a space (a saw kerf or ¹⁄₁₆ in) between pieces is a very good fit. This project has many small pieces and is difficult to fit. Begin with part A and B, then in order D, C, E, F, G, I, H, and J. Then continue one piece at a time to the back of the motorcycle. Fit and add the front end last.

7 Raise and lower pieces (p19) as pattern suggests. Raised areas marked with **R** has an additional ¼ in oak plywood.

    R   raised ¼ in   **L**   lower ¼ in
    R2 raised ³⁄₁₆ in   **L2** lower ³⁄₁₆ in
    R3 raised ³⁄₈ in

8 Make motor barrels using saw kerfs about ¹⁄₁₆ in deep, as shown. Make wheel spokes using crosscut saw kerfs about ¹⁄₁₆ in deep, as shown. Make kerf marks in transmission cover same as motor barrels.

9 Reassemble and mark on reference lines (p21). These lines will help with shaping. As you shape, round over to these lines (p21).

10 Assemble project onto backing material (p23). Trace around it, remove piece, and cut out the backing (p23). Reassemble project onto backing and prepare to glue.

11 Use ordinary white carpenter's glue. Glue up in the same order as suggested above for fitting. If backing material is flat, clamping should not be necessary. Keep all project pieces on backing board during glue-up. Carpenter's glue dries slowly so you will have 10 to 15 minutes to reposition pieces, if necessary, to achieve the best fit.

12 When thoroughly dried round over the backing edges (p24).

13 Cut out kickstand pattern piece. Drill ¼ in hole in back of the kickstand piece. Insert ¼ in dowel. Drill ¼ in hole in backing at X (shown on pattern, p80). Insert kickstand dowel in backing hole. The kickstand is used to support the motorcycle on a shelf or tabletop

Making motor barrels

1 Mark lines on motor barrel pattern piece.

2 Saw kerfs about ¹⁄₁₆ in deep.
3 Detail of finished motor barrel.

Left Insert and sand flush the alternate color dowel (white dowel in black part, black in white part).
Right Crisscross saw kerfs for wheel spokes

Making motorcycle kickstand

1 Cut out kickstand pattern piece and drill ¼ in hole in back of piece and insert ¼ in dowel.
2 Transfer X on pattern to backing and at the mark, drill ¼ in hole. *Do not* drill through the backing material.
3 Insert kickstand dowel into backing hole.

rather than hanging project on a wall.

14 Apply the finish (p25). Allow to dry.

Suggested shades of wood

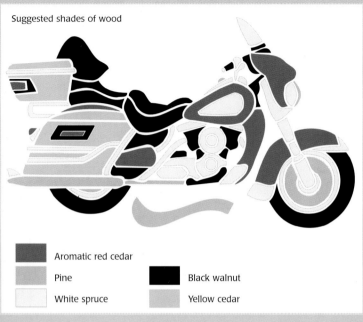

	Aromatic red cedar
	Pine
	White spruce
	Black walnut
	Yellow cedar

Suggested raising and lowering

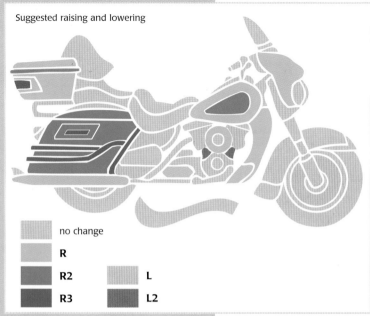

	no change
	R
	R2
	R3

	L
	L2

finished size 21 in x 12½ in

direction of wood grain

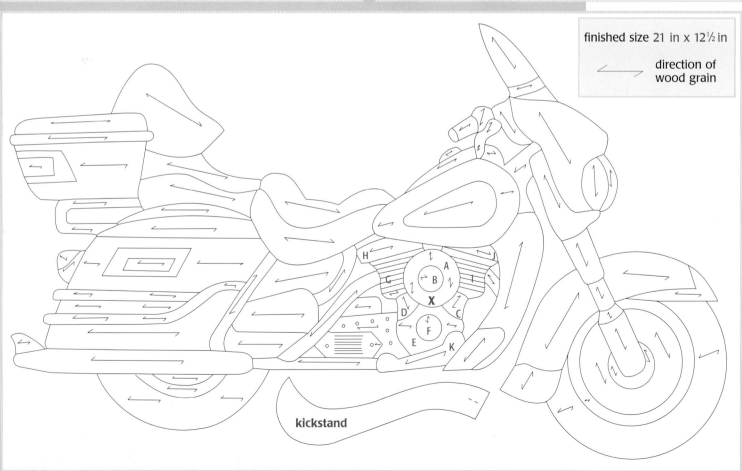

kickstand

Musical Note Clock

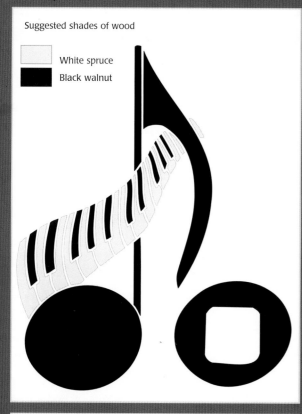

Suggested shades of wood

White spruce
Black walnut

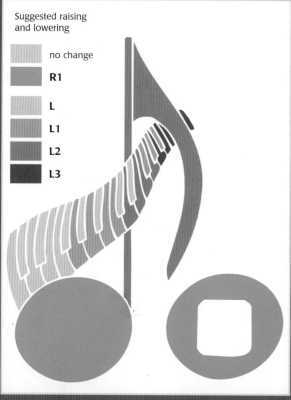

Suggested raising
and lowering

no change
R1
L
L1
L2
L3

No. of pieces 30
Finished size 8½ in x 14 in

Wood needed
White spruce (or Mississippi maple or holly) – 8 in x 5½ in
Black walnut (or very dark cedar) – 16 in x 5½ in

1 Enlarge (p15) the pattern on page 83 to the desired size. Make a template (p15) of the pattern. Clock may be made with a clock template (p86) and a standard battery clock movement. If using the template method, clock face "note" on pattern (p83) should be ¾ in thick. Rout out opening ½ in deep. This leaves a ¼ in face. Using a band saw, resaw ¼ in off face of note part. Cut out clock opening from the thickest part with a scroll saw. Glue face piece back on and sand the edges. See installing clock works, page 87.

2 Choose ¾-in thick wood, paying attention to grain direction marked on pattern.

3 Lay template pieces onto the wood shade or type as pattern suggests, and trace (p15) onto the wood.

4 Use a scroll saw and cut out with a #7 PGT type sharp blade. Make sure blade is square to the table (p12).

5 Cut out pieces carefully on the traced line. Make clock opening in note. Method 1 Rout out opening ½ in deep. Method 2 Resaw ½ in off note face with band saw. Cut out clock opening with scroll saw in this piece. Glue piece back on note. See page 87 for directions.

6 Assemble pieces on a lightbox (p18) and check fit. Pieces should fit together as closely as possible but a space (a saw kerf or ¹⁄₁₆ in) between pieces is acceptable.

7 The most difficult part of this project to fit is the keyboard. The tendency is to cut the pieces a bit large making the keyboard too long. As a precaution cut the pieces slightly small. The other three pieces are easy to fit.

8 Raise and lower pieces (p19) as pattern suggests.
R1   raise ¼ in   L   lower ⅛ in   L2 lower ⅜ in
                      L1 lower ¼ in   L3 lower ½ in

9 Reassemble pieces and mark on reference lines (p21). These lines will help with shaping. Shape and round over to these lines. Shape the note to have a definite rounded look.

10 Assemble project on the backing material (p23). Trace around it, remove pieces, and cut out the backing (p23). Be sure the hole in the backing is cut to match the clock opening in the note. Reassemble pieces on the cut-out back. Project is ready to glue.

11 Use ordinary white carpenter's glue. Glue note, staff, and flag first, then the keyboard. You may have to clamp the staff. Use a spring clamp and protect surface with a piece of scrap wood (p24). Keep all pieces of project on backing material during glue-up. Carpenter's glue will allow 10 to 15 minutes to reposition pieces, if necessary. Allow to dry.

12 Round over the backing edges (p24).

13 Apply the finish (p25). Allow to dry completely.

14 Attach the hanger (p25).

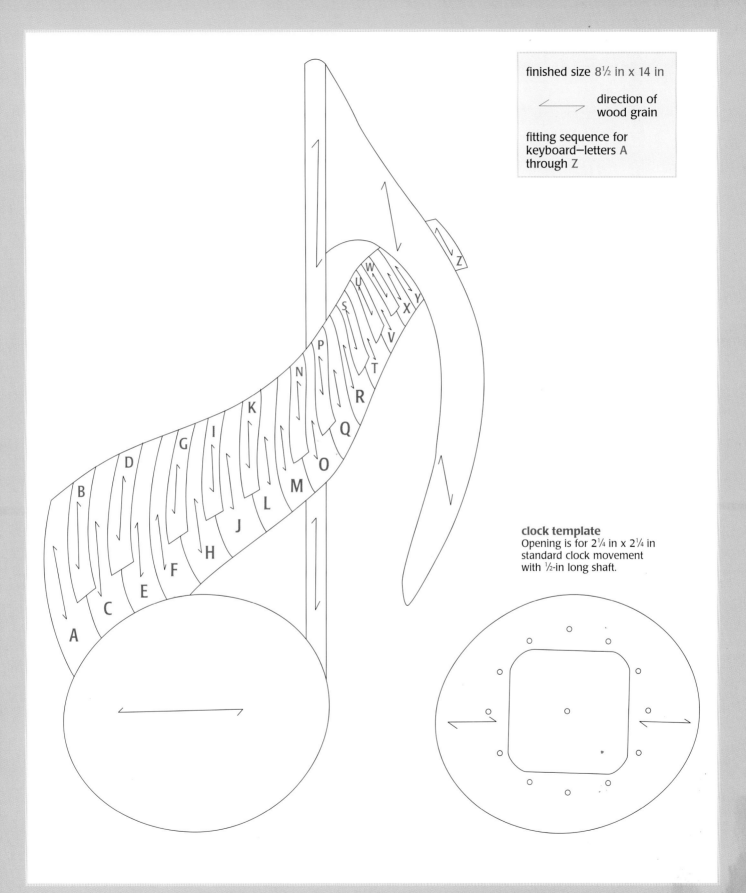

finished size 8½ in x 14 in

direction of
wood grain

fitting sequence for
keyboard–letters A
through Z

clock template
Opening is for 2¼ in x 2¼ in
standard clock movement
with ½-in long shaft.

Woodworker Clock

Above For a more exotic looking clock the following ½-in thick woods were substituted for those listed in the project.

    for hammer walnut and ash
    for chisel   red gum and osage
    for saw   Australian rosewood and pine
    for plane   red gum, walnut, and purple heart
    for blade clock face   Mississippi maple

No. of pieces 20
Finished size 16 in x 11 in

Wood needed
Light Western red cedar – 6 in x 3 in
Medium Western red cedar – 11 in x 4 in
Dark Western red cedar – 9 in x 5½ in
White spruce– 20 in x 5½ in

1 Enlarge (p15) the pattern on page 86 to the desired size. Make a template (p15) of the pattern.

2 Choose ¾-in thick wood, paying attention to grain directions as suggested on pattern.

3 Lay template pieces onto the wood shades or types as pattern suggests, and trace (p15) onto the wood.

4 Use a scroll saw and cut out with a #7 PGT style sharp blade. Make sure blade is square to the table (p12). Drill ³⁄₁₆ in hole at bottom of each saw tooth and then cut down to this hole. Cut out saw pieces after teeth have been cut from board, as shown.

5 Cut out pieces carefully on the traced line.

6 Assemble pieces on a lightbox (p18) and check fit. Pieces should fit together as closely as possible, but a space (a saw kerf or ¹⁄₁₆ in) between pieces is acceptable. Fit from the center out beginning with A in order through to T.

7 Raise and lower pieces (p19) as pattern suggests. Check for any rough edges, slivers, or high points and sand as needed.

R   raised ⅛ in   L   lower ⅛ in
                                 L1   lower ¼ in
                                 L2   lower ⅜ in
                                 L3   lower ½ in

8 Reassemble pieces and mark on reference lines (p21). These lines will help with shaping. Shape and round over to these lines. Round blade teeth edges slightly. Fully round the tool handles.

9 Assemble project on backing material (p23). Trace around it, mark center of clock on backing, remove pieces, and cut out the backing (p23). Using the clock hole template as a pattern trace clock opening on backing material. Cut out with scroll saw creating a recessed area for clock movement (p87). Drill a ⁷⁄₁₆ in hole in the center for the clock movement. A standard clock movement (used here) is 2¼ in x 2¼ in with a ⁷⁄₁₆ in shaft ½ in long. Reassemble project on the cut-out back and project is ready to glue.

10 Use ordinary carpenter's glue. Glue this project in the order of fitting, above. Clamp longer pieces such as H and M. Use spring clamps, and protect the surface with a piece of scrap wood (p24). Allow glue to dry for 30 minutes. Remove clamps and continue glue-up. Make sure all pieces of the project stay on the backing material during glue-up. Carpenter's glue will allow 10 to 15 minutes to reposition a piece, if necessary. Allow to dry.

11 Round over the backing edges (p24).

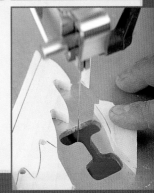

Making saw teeth
1 Drill ³⁄₁₆ in hole at the bottom of each tooth.
2 Using scroll saw, cut down to this hole.
3 Cut out saw pieces after teeth have been cut from board.

Left Drill hole for clock movement.   *Right* Clock parts

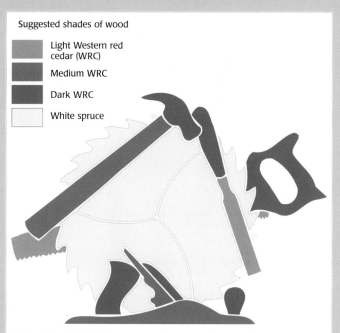

Suggested shades of wood

- Light Western red cedar (WRC)
- Medium WRC
- Dark WRC
- White spruce

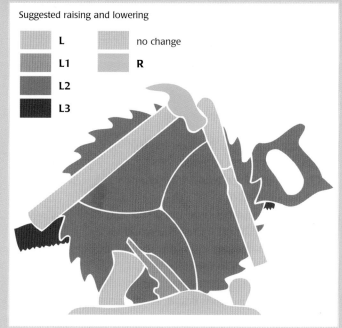

Suggested raising and lowering

- L
- L1
- L2
- L3
- no change
- R

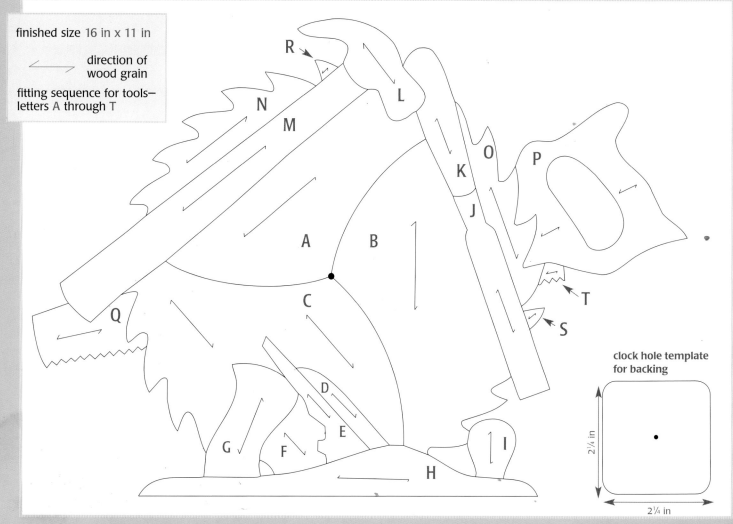

finished size 16 in x 11 in

direction of wood grain

fitting sequence for tools— letters A through T

clock hole template for backing

2¼ in

2¼ in

12. Attach the hanger (p25). **Note** Place a ⅜ in piece of wood under the hanger to move hanger out farther than the clock movement, as shown.

13. Apply the finish (p25). Allow to dry.

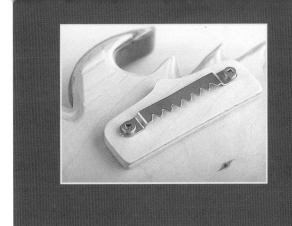

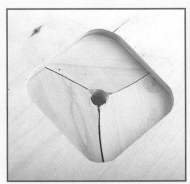

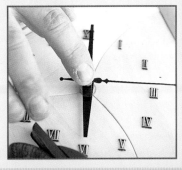

Installing Standard Clock Works

1. Using clock hole template from page 86, trace onto backing material. Cut out hole. When pieces are glued onto backing material this is how they should look. The recess in the back will receive clock movement.
2. Drill a ⁷⁄₁₆ in hole for the clock shaft.
3. Clock face "note" template on pattern (p83) will help lay out the numbers and opening for a standard 2¼ in x 2¼ in (with a ½ in long shaft) clock movement.
4. Use ⅜-in high Arabic numbers for best results.
5. Choose 1¾-in minute hand length, and brass spade hands.

Sports Clock

No. of pieces 56
Finished size 21 in x 14 in

Wood needed
Light Western red cedar – 6 in x 8 in
Medium light Western red cedar 6 in x 20 in
Medium Western red cedar – 2 in x 4 in
Medium dark Western red cedar – 2 in x 4 in
Dark Western red cedar – 6 in x 5 in
Blue spruce (choose piece with blue/gray marking in
    wood) – 6 in x 5 in
White aspen (or pine or spruce) – 6 in x 24 in
Black walnut (or very dark cedar) – 6 in x 12 in

1   Enlarge (p15) the pattern on page 90 to the desired
size. Make a template (p15) of the pattern.
2   Choose ¾-in thick wood, paying attention to grain
directions as marked on pattern.
3   Lay template pieces onto the wood shades or types as
pattern suggests, and trace (p15) onto the wood.
4   Use a scroll saw and cut out with a #7 PGT style sharp
blade. Make sure blade is square to the table (p12).
5   Cut out pieces carefully on the traced line. Cut kerf
marks in golf heads.
6   Assemble pieces on a lightbox (p18) and check fit.
Pieces should fit together as closely as possible, but a
space (a saw kerf or ¹⁄₁₆ in) between pieces is acceptable.
7   This project is a challenge to fit. Begin with the soccer
ball. Start with center A and fit through to O in order. Next
fit the baseball, the football, then the basketball. At this
time the hockey stick and puck will fit in nicely. Finally fit
the two golf clubs.
8   Raise and lower pieces (p19) as pattern suggests.
    R   raised ⅛ in   L   lower ⅛ in
    R1   raised ¼ in   L1   lower ¼ in
    R2   raised ⅜ in
    R3   raised ½ in
Check for rough edges, slivers, or high points. Sand smooth.
9   Reassemble pieces and mark on reference lines (p21).
These lines will help with shaping. The basketball is raised
quite high so there is sufficient wood to achieve a well-
rounded shape, which will be rounded over to the football.
Round football from the center out to the edges and do this
also with the soccer ball and baseball. This is a good project
to try a technique discussed in the shaping instructions
(p22). Temporarily glue pieces to a piece of scrap wood and
sand pieces as a unit. This produces a uniform shaping of
the balls, which should all be nicely rounded. Then remove
balls from scrap piece of wood and fit them into the project.
The stitching marks on the baseball are burned in with a
wood burning tool (p15). Curve iron head at an angle.

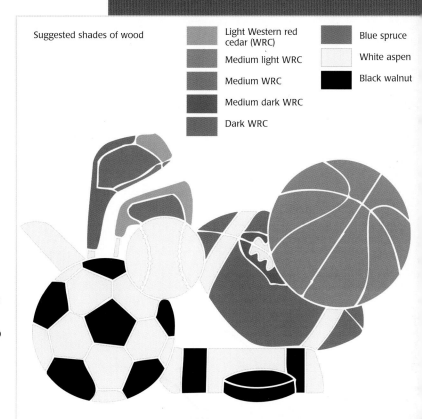

Suggested shades of wood

Light Western red cedar (WRC)
Medium light WRC
Medium WRC
Medium dark WRC
Dark WRC
Blue spruce
White aspen
Black walnut

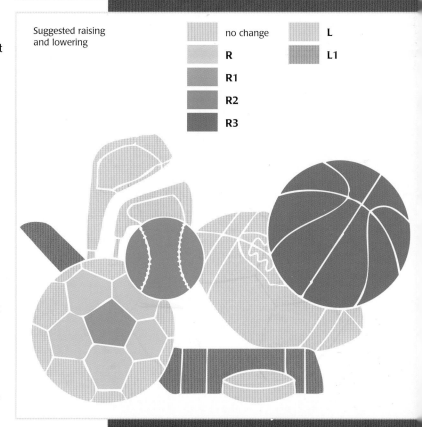

Suggested raising and lowering

no change
R
R1
R2
R3
L
L1

The clock movement is a standard clock insert style for a 3-in diameter hole. Hold pieces 1 and 2 together, draw on the circle, and cut out. For a small movement, adjust hole size.

10   Assemble project on ³⁄₈-in backing material (p23). Trace around it, remove pieces, and cut out backing (p23). Be sure to trace and cut out hole in backing for clock movement. Reassemble pieces on the cut-out back. Project is ready to glue.

11   Use ordinary white carpenter's glue. Begin with the soccer ball, then the basketball, football, baseball, hockey stick, and finally the golf clubs. Make sure the entire project stays completely on the backing material during glue-up. Carpenter's glue will allow 10 to 15 minutes to reposition a piece, if necessary. Allow to dry.

12   Round over the backing edges (p24).

13   Apply a durathane satin finish (p25). Allow to dry completely.

14   Attach the hanger (p25).

finished size 21 in x 14 in

⟷   direction of wood grain

⤳   slope down

fitting sequence for
soccer ball—letters A through O
basketball—numbers 1 to 8
footballl—letters A through M
baseballl—numbers 1 to 3
hockey stick and puck—letters A through H
golf clubs—numbers 1 to 9

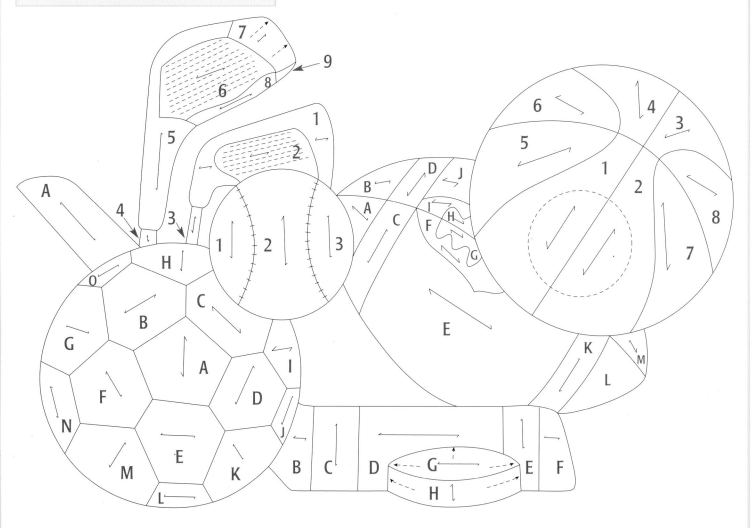

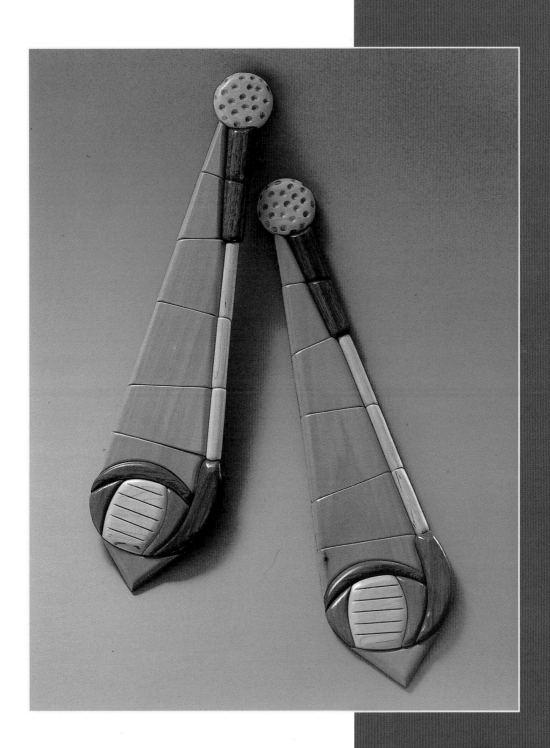

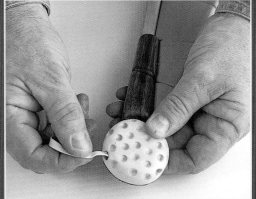

No. of pieces 18
Finished size 3 in x 18 in

Wood needed
Light Western red cedar − 4 in x 2 in
Medium Western red cedar − 4 in x 2 in
Dark Western red cedar − 5 in x 2 in
White pine (or Mississippi maple or holly) − 6 in x 6 in
Black walnut (or very dark cedar) − 5 in x 2 in
Green-cast American poplar (or sumac) − 15 in x 4 in

1 Enlarge (p15) the pattern on page 93 to the desired size. Make a template (p15) of the pattern.

2 Choose ¾-in thick wood, paying attention to grain directions as marked on pattern.

3 Lay template pieces onto the wood shades or types as pattern suggests.

4 Use a scroll saw and cut out with a #7 PGT style sharp blade. Make sure blade is square to the table (p12).

5 Cut out pieces carefully on the traced line. Cut kerf lines in club head, as shown on pattern.

6 Assemble pieces on a lightbox (p18) and check fit. Pieces should fit together as closely as possible, but a space (a saw kerf or ¹/₁₆ in) between pieces is acceptable.

7 Begin fitting this project from the bottom up. Fit the golf head pieces, then A, B, C and D; then E and F; G and H; I and J; and K and L. Finally fit in the golf ball.

8 Raise and lower pieces (p19) as pattern suggests.
R   raise ⅛ in
Check for any rough edges, slivers, or high points and sand as needed.

9 Reassemble pieces and mark on reference lines (p21). These lines will help with shaping. Shape and round over to these lines. Note that parts A, B, C, E, G, I, and K are kept flat except for the outside edges. The golf club is rounded down to the flat parts. To make the dimples on the golf ball knot, surface drill ¼ in holes about ¹/₁₆ in deep, as shown.

10 Instead of a wood backing this project is mounted on fabric backing. Fabric backing allows the tie to flex. The best material for the back is garment leather (vinyl is cheaper and easier to find, but not as strong). To attach tie around the neck, drill a ¼ in hole through the knot where marked with dotted lines. Use a piece of elastic (rubber band) about 16 in long x ¼ in wide. Glue velcro pieces on each end with velcro glue.

11 For this project, apply the finish (p25) to the pieces before applying glue.

12 Cut backing material oversize, glue pieces on using glue mentioned in note below and when glue has dried, trim material around project with a sharp knife.

Note The best glue for this project is a two-part epoxy. One-part epoxy or barge cement can be used but they are not preferred. Ordinary glue does not hold well.

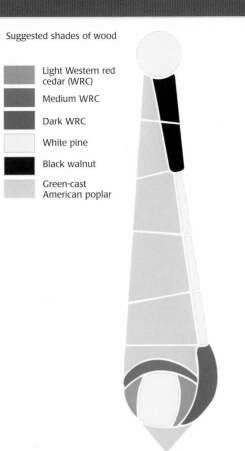

Suggested shades of wood

- Light Western red cedar (WRC)
- Medium WRC
- Dark WRC
- White pine
- Black walnut
- Green-cast American poplar

Suggested raising and lowering

- no change
- R

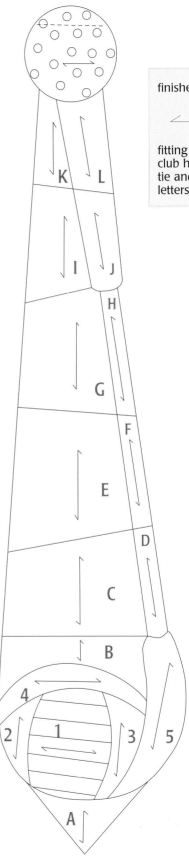

finished size 3 in x 18 in

direction of wood grain

fitting sequence for golf club head—numbers 1 to 5 tie and golf club shaft—letters A to L

Pricing Your Work

Garnet Hall has been a woodworker all his adult life. He began making furniture and toys on his small farm in rural Saskatchewan, Canada, during the winter off-season, but when he discovered intarsia in 1983 it became his main occupation. He has made and sold over 4000 pieces. Now he enjoys designing new patterns for intarsia work and developing new techniques for intarsia construction. His creative styles are available around the world and he writes articles for leading woodworking magazines. Currently he teaches intarsia and scroll saw classes. This is his first book on intarsia.

If you decide to sell your intarsia projects, you will have to determine a pricing schedule. What any craft/art piece is worth depends on a number of variables such as the quality of the workmanship, the relative affluence of the market area, and relative costs associated with the craft piece. As the intarsia crafter acquires more experience and skill, he or she can expect a higher price for their work. Belonging to a craft organization helps. They foster and encourage good craftsmanship and endeavor to educate the craft-buying public.

If the craftsperson/artist lives in a small town there will be less overhead but additional expenses to acquire wood. Those who have easy access to sawmills may be able to find wood at a cheaper price. All these factors should be considered in determining a price for your work. It's a good idea to keep a record of all expenses and time spent for each project. If you have many orders you can make more than one project at a time and this will save time and lower the price. It's easier and quicker to cut out twenty pieces at the same time, and shape and sand them together. You can also trace all the project pieces together, and fit all the pieces. To calculate individual time for multiple projects, take the entire time and divide it by the number of projects to get the average time for the individual project. Complex pieces or special orders will obviously be more time consuming and therefore more expensive. I charge $25 per hour, of which $11 covers marketing costs, materials, shop costs and other related expenses, and capital costs. This leaves $14 per hour for my time and effort. This is a good way to price objects for individual sales from you to the consumer.

Sometimes owners of small craft shops or art galleries will carry your work on consignment if they can't afford to buy the work outright. They will take 30 to 40 percent of the price for their trouble. This may seem like a large sum but the craftsperson won't have any market costs which includes booth fees, hotel rooms, meals, wear on vehicle, and gas. You will also gain production time. If the store buys outright, they will usually pay you 50 percent of the retail price. This leaves you with less money, but you will have the cash right away. Selling through stores involves some risk of non payment. Be cautious when you start and gradually build up a relationship. You will soon learn how stable the business is and the character of the owners. Another way to price your work is by the number of pieces in it. Using a scale of $3 to $3.50 per piece, a project that has twenty pieces would sell for 60 to 70 dollars. This formula is also helpful when someone asks you for a price on a commissioned piece.

Once you have set the price for an object, you can adjust it depending on the situation. If a particular piece consistently does not sell, stop making that item. If an item is very popular, increase the price by about 10 percent. It is a good idea to offer items in a variety of price ranges—from 20 to 100 dollars. Have a few pieces in the higher price range (100 dollars and over). The intricate pieces will attract attention to your booth and make the other pieces look more affordable. Expensive pieces sell best at juried shows. Flea markets and bazaars need less expensive price ranges. Try to put a realistic price on your hard work. The projects you make and sell deserve a fair price.

Pricing your craft/art piece depends on quality of workmanship, relative affluence of market area, and costs such as materials and time involved.

Index